Louise Hampden has had a lifelong interest in gardening. After qualifying in horticulture and garden design at Berkshire College of Agriculture she started her own garden design business and has since been involved in several gardening programmes. She has worked on *Gardeners' World* over the last ten years, starting as a researcher, and she is the current producer of the programme.

10 9 8 7 6 5 4 3 2

BBC Books, an imprint of Ebury Publishing
20 Vauxhall Bridge Road,
London SW1V 2SA

BBC Books is part of the Penguin Random House group of companies
whose addresses can be found at global.penguinrandomhouse.com

Penguin
Random House
UK

First published by Woodland Books in 2008
This edition published by Woodland Books in 2019

www.penguin.co.uk

A CIP catalogue record for this book is available from the British Library

ISBN 9781785944932

Commissioning editor: Lorna Russell
Project editor: Caroline McArthur
Copy-editor: Caroline Taggart
Designer: Smith & Gilmour
Production controller: Helen Everson

Printed and bound in Great Britain by Clays Ltd, Elcograf S.p.A.

Penguin Random House is committed to a sustainable future for
our business, our readers and our planet. This book is made
from Forest Stewardship Council® certified paper.

**Gardeners'
World**

TOP TIPS

A Treasury of Garden Wisdom

Louise Hampden

BOOKS

CONTENTS

CHAPTER ONE

FLOWER POWER

*If gardening doesn't teach us anything else it should teach us faith.
All the time we are shivering and complaining nature is working
miracles underground. I die a hundred deaths until I see all my
friends coming back to greet me, but I needn't worry; nearly always
they come through safe and sound, but I never feel completely safe
till I see those thrusting shoots of pink or green or grey.*

MARGERY FISH
A Flower for Every Day

SPRING

*The truth about the majority of spring-flowering trees and shrubs is
that they last in beauty for one week only. Almond, plum, cherry and
apple blossom come and go with alarming fleetness, each leaving us
with another fifty-one weeks of waiting for its return; and yet we do
not look at the matter like that at all. For when they burst into our
consciousness and are vividly with us, their presence carries
us forward to spring's next revelation and then the next.*

CHRISTOPHER LLOYD
The Well-Tempered Garden

Spring is that arbitrary word that signals that winter is over.
It's a time of black twigs, bare mud and brave buds gingerly
breaking the surface of the soil. For the gardener it is the
most exciting time of the year: along with the sap, we rise
and leap into action. But it is also a tricky time, often going
from freezing rain, snow and frost to warm, balmy t-shirt
days. The knack with spring is to know what the plants are
up to and to garden only at the right time.

THE NOVICE GARDENER needs to know that you can't
start sowing and planting everything just because it is 21 March.
Gardening at this time of year is mostly about tidying up and
preparing for warmer weather. No matter what it says on the
seed packet, it's best to hold off planting even if there is a warm
spell. Plants want to grow, but they grow when *they* want to.
They respond to changing light and heat levels, but not much
grows above ground until temperatures consistently reach
around 7°C and above, and the days grow longer. Early bulbs
appear because the temperature is higher below ground than
above it.

AS SOON AS THE SOIL is no longer waterlogged or frozen and has dried out from the winter wet, it's time to tidy up the borders. Remove any dead leaves, take out any weeds and lightly fork over the surface of the soil, adding compost or well-rotted manure to improve the condition of the soil and feed the plants.

ANOTHER TASK YOU CAN PERFORM early in spring is dividing herbaceous perennials. When a plant is called herbaceous, it means that the stems are soft or succulent and green, as opposed to brown and woody like shrubs and trees. Soft, green, herbaceous growth will generally die back to the ground in cold winter climates. The roots remain alive under the soil and new growth emerges in the spring. You can start dividing in late summer to early winter while the soil is still warm. Only the hardiest plants can be divided in the cold winter months.

TOP TIP

Buy large pots of perennials as these can often be divided straight away, making three small plants instead of one large one.

DIVIDING PERENNIALS is one of the easiest ways to get plants for free; it is also an essential maintenance task for older perennials, as they often become woody, flower less and die out from the centre. Instant rejuvenation begins by digging up the plant and breaking it up into pieces, keeping the newer growth and discarding the central, woody bit. Most plants can just be pulled apart by hand. Washing the roots first in a bucket of water and swishing it about a bit gets rid of some of the clinging soil and makes division easier; it also helps you pick out the best young roots.

If the plant is too unwieldy to pull apart manually, then a handy trick is to dig it up, place it on a piece of hessian to protect any surface (such as the grass), insert two garden forks through the middle of the plant back to back and then lever it apart.

For smaller but tough plants like hostas, wash the roots as above and cut through the plant using a sharp knife.

Plant any divisions immediately, replenishing the soil with some compost or well-rotted manure, and water in very well. Nurture the plants along by regular watering, especially if there is a dry spell.

HOW DO PLANTS KNOW THAT IT IS SPRING?

Plants have evolved strategies to keep from being 'fooled' into thinking that it is spring before it really is. So even if we experience a warm spell in late winter or early spring, they won't suddenly spurt into growth and put out leaves. That is because plants native to temperate regions need a season of low temperatures followed by a period when day lengths are longer than in winter in order to grow. They also have chilling requirements: the number of hours that a plant must be exposed to temperatures between 0°C and 7°C before they start to grow again. (The times when the temperature drops below 0°C or rises above 7°C do not count.) Incredibly, plants are somehow able to keep track of the number of hours they are exposed to this very specific range of temperature. Apples, for example, need between 1000 and 1400 hours at about 7°C before they start their spring growth.

SOME SPRING FLOWERS such as forsythia and witch hazel (*Hamamelis*), open before their leaves because they are making themselves more visible to pollinating insects and getting the reproductive process off to an early start. They form their flower buds in the latter part of the previous year before going dormant as a response to shortening day lengths.

DON'T BUY PLANTS TOO EARLY in the spring, as they won't be growing of their own accord: they will most likely have been brought into flower in a nice warm polytunnel somewhere. You will then plonk them into a patch of cold mud, where they will sit waiting for certain death. It will be like lying in a bikini in the garden on a winter's day. Let the nurseries and garden centres nurture the plants for a few more weeks until the weather and the soil warm up.

WHEN BUYING A CONTAINER-GROWN PLANT, don't be afraid to tap it out of its pot to examine the roots. If they look fresh and white, if they fill the pot and are not curling around the bottom, the plant is growing well. Don't buy a plant that has no visible roots, as the chances are that it has just been repotted and you'll be paying a lot for a small plant in a big pot of compost.

> ### TOP TIP
> *Don't buy plants from a nursery or garden
> centre if the pot has weeds or moss growing on it.
> The plant will have been in the pot too long
> and will be pot-bound.*

WHEN THE TEMPERATURE GAUGE LEAPS UP and it starts to feel consistently warmer, most hardy plants are ready for planting. They are just starting to come out of their winter dormancy, the soil in the garden is moist and warming up and, consequently, the plants' roots will soon grow away and take up nutrients from the soil. Let nature tell you when to plant. Look at what's happening outside: if most established plants are starting to grow, it's warm enough to put new ones into the soil.

PLANTING IN SPRING

You can plant trees, shrubs and perennials at any time of year, except when the soil is frozen or waterlogged, as long as they are container-grown. This is because most plants we buy from the garden centre or nurseries have been grown in containers

THE COMING OF SPRING

In 1736 Robert Marsham began the series of records that he
developed into 27 'Indications of Spring'. These included
flowering dates of four species and leafing dates of 13 trees; the
arrival or first song of migrant birds and signs of the breeding
activity of rooks, frogs and toads. Marsham looked out for the
first snowdrops, first swallows and butterflies, listened for the
first cuckoos and noted the dates on which he first saw or heard
them each year. This activity is called phenology.

On Marsham's death in 1797, the Indications of Spring were
continued by successive members of his family, right down until
1958. They represent the longest such record in the UK and have
been inspirational in phenological recording ever since. These
records are hugely important today, as scientists need to know
how nature responds to climate change in order to predict the
consequences for the future and, to that end, thousands of
people across the UK actively monitor the seasons within the
phenology network.

The Marsham records show us just how responsive spring
events are to temperature: a difference of as little as 1°C (1.8°F)
can bring a plant into leaf eight days earlier. Not all species
respond at the same rate, however — hawthorn, for example,
is very responsive to warming, beech less so.

and spent all their life in pots of varying sizes, so their roots are
completely self-contained. Plants that have just been dug out
of the ground whilst in active growth are less likely to survive.

THE SECRET OF PLANTING ANYTHING is to
make sure that the soil is well prepared, the roots are firmed
in properly and the plant is watered well before and after
planting. Never plant a dry plant.

WHEN PLANTING A CONTAINER-GROWN PLANT
dig a hole twice as wide and slightly deeper than the container.
Add a couple of spadesful of compost or organic matter to the
soil you have dug out, mix it up and then put a spadeful of this
mixture back in the bottom of the hole. Hold the plant with
one hand over the top of the compost to support it, taking care
not to damage any emerging shoots, then turn it upside down
and tap the bottom of the pot. The plant should come out
easily, but with a plastic pot a gentle squeeze sometimes helps.
Position the plant in the centre of the hole. Make sure the
top of the compost is level with the surrounding soil and
then fill in the gaps at the sides with the soil mixture. Firm
the soil gently around the plant, leaving no gaps or air pockets
(this is called 'firming in') and finally water well.

TOP TIP
In dry weather, or in summer, it often helps
to water the hole before placing the plant in it.
This ensures that the water goes where it is
needed — to the roots.

MULCH IS A WORD often used but rarely explained: it
simply means materials placed on top of the soil to keep weeds
down, reduce water loss and protect the soil's surface. Most mulch
will also improve the structure of the soil, as earthworms will soon
get to work and pull the material down into the soil. (For more
about the importance of soil structure, see page 169.)

Lots of different materials can be used for mulching.
Mushroom compost, spent hops and even straw will condition
the soil, but will not be a source of nutrients for the plants,

so by far the best material is homemade, weed-free compost or well-rotted manure — about two bucketsful to each square metre of soil. Mulching is best carried out in the spring, because the soil is moist underneath and a mulch will act as a blanket, keep the soil moist and reduce evaporation.

BULBS

The cultivation of bulbs can bring much happiness and colour into the life of the cultivator. There is a great sense of achievement in contemplating a garden, or for that matter a house, which is decorated with home-grown blooms. Most of the colours are bright and gay and considerably help to dispel the gloom of wintry days.

M JAMES
The Complete Guide to Homes and Gardens

The spring garden would be nothing without the bright yellows of daffodils, the blues of scillas, the scent of hyacinths and the myriad colours of tulips. They are the Pot Noodles of the horticultural world. Plant in the autumn (see page 50 for more about how to do that), add time and water, and up they pop to illuminate the garden. A bulb is next year's plant neatly packaged and surrounded by scale leaves, immature leaves, flower stems and sometimes even flower buds. The whole bulb is often wrapped, as with daffodils and tulips, in a papery brown tunic.

> **TOP TIP**
> *When buying bulbs, choose the largest
> and firmest available.*

LEAVES OF DAFFODILS and other bulbs often seem to be a problem for the tidy gardener, yet they are the most important part of the plant. The leaves will be around for at least six weeks, drawing energy from the spring sunshine to make next year's flowers, so *leave the leaves*.

If you really can't bear to see the leaves, and space is at a premium, grow the bulbs in pots and place them around the garden when they are in flower. When they have finished, put them out of sight to die down naturally.

DAFFODILS EPITOMIZE SPRING and need to be planted from September onwards. Small varieties are best and don't fall over like the big ones.

TULIPS ARE THE MOST
COLOURFUL FLOWERS
of the late spring border and
there are varieties that will flower
from February through to late
May. They also make a good
cut flower. Plant them from
October but preferably not until
November, as they are prone to
a virus called tulip fire if planted
too early. Carry on planting even
into December. If you plant
tulips deeply in the vegetable
patch, you can then plant early
cabbages and other vegetables
between the rows; very soon the
dying foliage of the tulips will be
covered by expanding vegetables.

A BIT OF TULIP HISTORY

Tulips originated on the hot, dry hillsides of Europe, the Middle East and Asia. The name comes from a corruption of the Persian *thoulyban* or *tulipant*, meaning 'turban', which the flower was thought to resemble. The story of tulip cultivation starts with an Antwerp merchant receiving some bulbs with a consignment of cloth from Turkey, who cooked and ate them assuming they were onions. The Romans mashed them and used them as corn plasters, but for western Europeans they were to become extremely valuable.

Tulips were first planted in Holland by Carolus Clusius, head botanist at the Leiden Botanic Garden at the end of the sixteenth century. He was very stingy with the bulbs, refusing to give any away or even to sell any. Some people saw the potential of making money with them, but Clusius wouldn't play. Eventually part of the collection was stolen and the Dutch cultivation of tulips began, slowly but surely, in private plots.

When tulips first came on the market they were a rarity that only the wealthy could afford and they soon became a status symbol – aristocrats all over Europe had to have them and the buying mania took off. By 1624 the craze was at its peak with a 'broken ' tulip – that is, a solid colour with veining – called Semper Augustus commanding 3000 guilders per bulb, with only 12 available for sale. By 1634 people were trading houses, businesses, ships and farms for bulbs. Tulips were bought before they were out of the ground – so-called 'wind trading' – and people also borrowed huge sums to speculate.

The bubble (or bulb!) burst when a decree passed on 27 April 1637 declared that bulbs were products, not investments, and were to be paid for in cash. Thousands of people went bankrupt, tax revenues plummeted and the Dutch army and navy had to be drastically reduced. The long-term result was the loss of several colonies, including New Amsterdam, which was renamed New York by the British when they captured it in the 1640s.

PLANTS THAT WON'T LET
YOU DOWN IN SPRING

Trees and Shrubs

The flowering currant (*Ribes sanguineum*) is one of the first shrubs of spring, hanging its dark pink flowers on naked stems before the leaves appear. To keep it in check, cut out any old stems and a few flowering stems immediately after it has finished flowering.

Japanese flowering cherry (*Prunus*) comes in many varieties and is a valuable small tree for gardens, smothered in pink or white double flowers — it epitomizes a warm spring day.

Star magnolia (*Magnolia stellata*) has waxy white flowers on naked stems and is an ideal small tree for front gardens.

Viburnums (*Viburnum* spp.) are tough plants for fairly shady places. Many spring-flowering varieties have clusters of highly scented white flowers that can fill a garden with perfume.

Perennials and Bulbs

Tulips (*Tulipa* spp.): from elegant white lily-shaped flowers to garish bright colours, you can have a tulip in flower in the garden from late March to the end of May.

Daffodils (*Narcissus* spp.) epitomize spring and can be in flower from February to May, depending on the variety.

Primroses (*Primula vulgaris*) has tiny yellow flowers that emerge from the centre of a crowd of leaves to herald the start of spring. Plant at the front of borders for full enjoyment.

Wallflowers (*Cheiranthus cheiri*) can fill a garden with scent on a warm spring day and, planted with bulbs like daffodils and tulips, will hide the dying foliage of bulb leaves.

Columbine (*Aquilegia* spp.) is a classic cottage-garden plant. It is easy to grow, seeds itself around and is covered with nodding heads of flowers from April to mid June. This plant takes the garden from late spring into summer.

Spurge (*Euphorbia* spp.). Who can resist the bright yellow bracts, which light up the spring border and persist well into summer?

Ornamental onions (*Allium* spp.) are topped in early summer with balls of white, to cornflower blue and purple.

THE LAWN

Cutting the grass is like an instant makeover for the garden. No matter whether the borders are rampant with weeds or beautifully tended, a well-cut, crisply edged lawn will show off the best and hide the worst. Grass starts to grow madly in spring and it is a good idea to give it its first cut sooner rather than later. Don't cut too close at first, though — a light trim to take down the height to about 4 cm is sufficient. Otherwise it will be scalped, making bare patches, and, as nature abhors a vacuum, weeds will soon fill the space.

LAWNS ARE SIMPLY lots of individual plants grown together; cutting the grass encourages each little plant to bush out and thicken, as does each subsequent cut, so it is far better for the lawn to cut a little and often. But, at *Gardeners' World*, we don't let the lawn rule our gardening life. As a living, breathing plant it deserves our best care, but we don't mind clover or daisies. We grub up dandelions and other tap-rooted weeds, feed with an organic fertilizer and then cut it regularly throughout the summer. We re-seed bare patches and repair edges as the need arises, but we don't water it in drought, as we know that within a week of a good downpour it will be green again.

TO IMPROVE THE LOOK OF A LAWN either in early spring or at the end of the summer, it is sometimes necessary to grab a spring-tined rake, a fork, a broom, some lawn seed and a few buckets of sand and get ready for some hard exercise.

First rake over the lawn, scratching the surface with the spring tines. This will bring up bits of grass, moss and other debris called 'thatch'. Take this away and then prick over the whole area with a border fork, wiggling the prongs about to make small holes.

Lawns love sand, sand and more sand, so spread it over the lawn, brushing it in and working it into the holes.

Finally, sprinkle the lawn seed over any bare patches and water it in. The lawn will recover from this drastic treatment within a couple of weeks and spring back into action with more vigour.

——— SOME FACTS ABOUT LAWNS ———

The lawn is more than just the sum of its parts. The smell of freshly cut grass in spring tops the list of the most pleasant and comforting smells and, in experiments, it has been shown that standing barefoot on grass can trigger a reduction in the signs of stress: both heart rate and blood pressure have been shown to fall. A lawn has a tremendous cooling effect. On a hot summer's day its surface can be at least 16.5°C cooler than that of tarmac.

A lawn cleans itself by taking in garden debris and organic matter. Not only does it trap and filter dust and dirt from the air, it can also reduce pollution by purifying the water passing through its root zone. Grass is one of the major producers of new soil by growing, dying off, decomposing and redeveloping. By leaving clippings on the lawn and allowing them to decay naturally, you return a significant amount of nutrients to the lawn to help it grow and build topsoil.

Dense, healthy grass is the best natural surface for trapping water and reducing soil erosion. A lawn of 200 square metres can absorb over 4500 litres of rainwater without noticeable run-off. One of the main causes of urban flooding over recent years is the removal of lawns to make room for car parking or hard-surface landscaping. Rainwater is no longer slowly absorbed, but runs off into the street and overloads the drains.

Water absorbed by a lawn nourishes grass, trees, shrubs and flowers before filtering through the topsoil and replenishing groundwater supplies.

LAWN CARE IN HISTORY

The lawn has been an important part of gardens in Europe since the Middle Ages. A fourteenth-century work called *Opus ruralium commodorum* ('The Advantages of Country Living') gave this advice for preparing a lawn:

Dig out all the weeds and roots.
Scald the soil with boiling water to prevent further weeds germinating.
Dig up sods from the wild and lay.
Beat with wooden mallets or 'beetles' [still used today] and tread with the feet until the grass is almost invisible.
Fresh growth should appear.
Aftercare was to cut the sward twice a year.

The French *Maison Rustique* of 1564 added to this advice. After the initial preparation as above, turves should be placed grass side downwards 'and afterward daunced upon with the feete, and the beater or pauing beetle lightly passing ouer them, in such sort as that within a short time after, the grass may begin to peepe up and put foorth like small haires; and finallie it is made the sporting greenplot for Ladies and Gentelwomen to recreate their spirits in.'

SUMMER

*Even the dullest garden can't help being colourful in June. When the
cow parsley reaches shoulder level in the hedgerows and the roadside
is scented with honeysuckle and wild roses, the garden too seems to
grow up overnight. This is the time when one discovers if one has
planted too closely, and I always have, and if one has staked
sufficiently and efficiently, and I never have.*

MARGERY FISH
A Flower for Every Day

ROSES

*The beauty of the rose is not confined to what we see: it is also one of the
most fragrant of flowers. Its fragrance lifts our spirits as few others can.*

DAVID AUSTIN
The English Roses

Roses are the highlight of the summer garden for many people.
The different classifications can be a bit confusing, but the
very basics you need to know are:

HYBRID TEA ROSES have the archetypal 'chocolate box'
shape and can be good for cutting. They bear large flowers that
commonly grow one to a long stem and bloom continually
throughout the growing season. The bush can grow quite tall
and upright and be rather twiggy. Hybrid teas do best if they
are pruned almost to the ground in spring.

SHRUB ROSES are generally large plants and most,
particularly modern ones such as the English roses, bloom

profusely throughout the season. If you want to fill a large space with colour, the shrub category offers great choice.

OLD ROSES are made up of many subclasses, including alba, bourbon, China, hybrid perpetual, damask, rugosa and species roses. Many old roses bloom only once during the growing season but some, particularly rugosa, produce large and colourful hips once flowering is over.

CLIMBERS produce long stems that must be anchored to a fence, trellis or other support. Flowers will appear along the length of a stem that is trained horizontally. Some climbers bloom only once in the summer, but many modern varieties produce flowers throughout the growing season.

RAMBLERS are like climbers but are much more vigorous in growth and have vicious hooks for thorns. They can often grow up into the canopy of trees and so are useful for adding interest in a large space. They flower only once in a season, with clusters of small flowers.

IF YOU ABSOLUTELY MUST HAVE a once-flowering old rose, plant a late-flowering clematis to grow through it: the clematis will then flower when the rose doesn't. (For a lot more about clematis, see page 150).

A BIT OF ROSE HISTORY

Fossilized rose flowers and hips that are reckoned to be 35 million years old have been found in Europe, and petrified rose wreaths have been unearthed from ancient Egyptian tombs.

The earliest documented evidence of the rose is found in Homer's epic *The Iliad,* which was composed some time in the ninth century BC. Homer writes that Achilles carried a shield decorated with roses. He killed the Trojan prince Hector, whose body was anointed in rose oil before being embalmed by the goddess Aphrodite, to whom the rose is dedicated. According to myth it was Aphrodite who caused roses to be red. Upon seeing her lover Adonis mortally wounded she ran to him and in her haste scratched herself on the thorns of some roses, which up until this time had always been white. As her blood fell on the white blooms they became stained, ever more to remain red. The Romans, turning Aphrodite into their goddess Venus, also adopted the rose and it became the symbol of love and beauty, as it still is today.

One of our earliest cultivated roses was the *Rosa gallica,* which is richly scented and has pink or red petals. It was grown by the ancient Greeks and the Romans, who both used it to make perfume. When the Roman emperor Nero showered his dinner guests with rose petals they were probably from gallicas.

The best known gallica variety is *Rosa gallica officinalis,* the apothecary's rose, named after its medieval use in making perfume and medicine. It is also called the red damask, after the city of Damascus, for it may have been brought to England by crusaders returning from the Holy Land.

Another early rose variety was the white *Rosa alba,* a cross between a gallica and a dog rose (*R. canina*). In the Middle Ages, the alba was adopted by the Christian Church as a symbol of the Virgin Mary, its whiteness symbolizing her purity.

TOP TIP

If you have a small garden, look for roses that flower all summer long, as a rose that takes up a lot of space for one month of glory can be disappointing.

ROSES ARE HUNGRY PLANTS and the secret of success lies in great soil preparation, digging over the area to be planted and adding lots of well-rotted manure or compost.

BY FAR THE CHEAPEST WAY to buy roses, and the easiest way to plant them, is bare root, which means that they have been lifted from the fields where they were growing late in the autumn, when all their leaves have fallen off. Bare-root roses are bought mail order from rose growers; order them from summer onwards and they will be dispatched any time from November to February, depending on weather conditions. Because they are dormant, they will not die in the post. Sometimes the weather is too frosty and cold for them to be planted as soon as they arrive, so they can remain in their packing for up to a week. If after that time weather conditions are still unsuitable, unwrap the plants and place in a container of damp sand or soil.

PLANTING A BARE-ROOT ROSE. Never plant a rose when its roots are dry, nor during frost. Soak the roots in a bucket of water overnight before planting. Next day, dig a hole large enough for the roots to be spread out and deep enough for the soil to be 7.5 cm above the point where the roots meet the growth. Work the soil in between the roots and fill in the hole gently, firming with your feet. Bare-root roses are usually pruned before they are sent out; if not, they need to be cut down to a height of about 45cm.

EVERYBODY DREADS ROSE PRUNING but it is not that complicated. Just remember the three Ds. First, prune out dead, diseased and dying wood, ruthlessly and down to the ground. Most modern roses grown as shrubs can then be cut back to a third of their height, though some species roses only need to be pruned to get rid of the 3Ds and to remove older wood which won't produce many flowers. Then thin the rose out by taking out any weak and twiggy bits, leaving an open shape with no branches crossing over each other. Late winter, when there are no leaves on the branches and it is easy to see the framework of the plant, is the best time for rose pruning. February and March are traditionally regarded as the best months but, as with most gardening tasks, this is not a hard and fast rule. Pruning in January is just as effective.

A ROSE IN THE WRONG PLACE can be moved, but prune it back hard first, taking out a lot of the old wood and leaving younger and greener wood. Dig it up with as much soil around the roots as possible and re-plant immediately, taking care not to break up the rootball. Water it in well and keep watering regularly until it gets going.

CLIMBING ROSES WILL FLOWER BETTER
if the branches are trained horizontally. This is because the plant naturally wants to grow upwards but, if you bend the branch horizontally, the hormones that are normally concentrated just at the tip are now spread equally along the stem, encouraging each bud to break into leaf and later produce a flower.

DON'T FORGET TO DEAD-HEAD ROSES once the flowers fade to encourage them to keep flowering. This is effective for all roses except those, like the old roses, that flower only once. Roses grown for their colourful hips should not be dead-headed, as the flowers need to be left on the plant to form the hips in the autumn.

Roses that are thoroughly good 'doers'

Hybrid teas: Mrs Oakley Fisher, Peace
Shrub roses: Buff Beauty, Gertrude Jekyll, Graham Thomas
Climbers: Ena Harkness. Blairii Number 2, New Dawn
Old and species roses: *Rosa mutabilis*, Charles de Mills, Blanc Double de Coubert
Rambler: Wedding Day, Alberic Barbier
Roses for hips: *Rosa rugosa* 'Alba', *Rosa* 'Geranium'

TOP TIP
Shrubby roses with long shoots which flower only at the tips can also be encouraged to make more flowers by pegging and tying the long shoots down to the ground.

ANNUALS

Many annuals have a quality of gaiety and freshness that is especially gladdening, I find. 'Here we are,' they seem to say; 'enjoy us while you may. We cannot stay for long.'

CHRISTOPHER LLOYD
The Well-Tempered Garden

One of the easiest plants to grow is an annual, which is a flower that is sown, grows, flowers, produces seed and then dies – all in one year. Within 12 weeks of sowing, an annual will be flowering its socks off. The secret of success with annuals is understanding that its sole purpose in life is to perpetuate itself by making seed – so if you dead-head it regularly it will keep on making more flowers in a desperate attempt to produce seed.

THE GREAT THING ABOUT ANNUALS is that it doesn't matter if you sow them late – they will just flower later. As long as they have 12 weeks in which to grow and flower, they will do so.

THE BEST TIME TO SOW is in spring, as soon as weeds start to grow in the garden – then the soil will be warm enough. Don't sow seed in winter – it will rot and never grow. You can also plant 'hardy annuals' such as marigolds and cornflowers in the autumn. They are tough enough to stand winter temperatures, often making quite stocky plants before the onset of winter and beginning to flower in late spring.

WHAT AN ANNUAL NEEDS is a sunny part of the garden where it is not overcrowded by other plants. It likes soil that is not too rich, that has not been recently manured and, for sowing, that has been finely raked over. To get the right texture, dig over the soil to a spade's depth, bash it down with the back of a fork until it starts to look a bit finer and then get raking, bashing down the larger crumbs and raking again until the soil looks like biscuit crumbs.

IT'S NOT DIFFICULT TO SOW SEED. Just remember that a tiny seed does not need 30 cm of soil over the top of it. It needs a fine covering, plus enough warmth and moisture to get going.

ANNUAL SEEDS ARE BEST SOWN IN ROWS. The reason for this is not an aesthetic one. If you don't know what the seedling looks like, it makes absolute sense to sow in rows; then you can tell seedlings from weedlings. On *Gardeners' World* we often sow in circles, arcs and crosses, sometimes using a bottle of sand to mark out the shapes. Weed seedlings will pop up randomly, whereas the annual seedlings will be in the defined shapes we sowed. Once the plants have been thinned out and have grown bigger the regimented shapes disappear.

ANNUALS ARE PERFECT for 'new build' homes where the garden has not been a consideration. For a few pounds, packets of annuals sown in spring will produce an 'instant' garden and plenty of cut flowers for the house.

ANY GAP IN A SUNNY SPOT can be filled with annuals grown on in pots. Sprinkle a few seeds over a pot of compost, thin out to three seedlings per pot and plant them out once they have a good root system.

ONE OF THE BEST ANNUALS for cut flowers is the sweet pea, which can be grown in the open ground or in containers as long as it has a strong support to climb up.

TOP TIP

Sow annuals for cut flowers as the more you pick the more flowers you get.

Sweet pea seeds have quite a tough coating and can be hard to germinate, but try placing them on a saucer on top of a piece of soaked kitchen towel for a couple of days – they soon start to sprout. At this point they can be planted individually into pots and placed in a sheltered spot to grow on a bit.

Failsafe Annuals

Love-in-a-mist (*Nigella damascena*)

Californian poppies (*Eschscholzia californica*)

Cornflowers (*Centaurea cyanus*)

Larkspur (*Delphinium consolida*)

Poached egg plant (*Limnanthes douglasii*)

Ladybird poppy (*Papaver* 'Ladybird')

Opium poppy (*Papaver somniferum*)

SWEET PEAS DON'T LIKE
their roots being disturbed and are often grown in biodegradable pots so that they can be planted out still inside the pot. When they are a few centimetres high and ready to be planted out in late spring, 'nip out' the tops (just pinch the tip off with your fingers) so that the plant branches out. Sweet peas can also be sown in autumn in pots, overwintered in a cold frame and planted out in spring.

SWEET PEAS MUST BE PICKED DAILY. This is one annual that will stop flowering immediately if it is allowed to produce pods. The more you pick the more flowers you get.

SWEET PEA HISTORY

The sweet pea is native to Southern Italy. A Sicilian monk, Franciscus Cupani, sent seeds to Dr Robert Uvedale of Enfield in 1699. The seed was of a purple/maroon bicolour which is still often sold by the name 'Cupani' or 'Matucana'. Its flowers are small, but fabulously fragrant. Variations on this original appeared throughout the eighteenth century, and the nineteenth century saw a slow improvement in its popularity until Henry Eckford, a Scot living in Shropshire, bred the grandiflora strain with larger flowers in a range of colours. These retained the scent of the original, while greatly enhancing its ornamental value.

Eckford's claim to fame was cemented when one of his finest varieties, the pink 'Prima Donna', mutated on three separate occasions. In each case the form of the flower was dramatically altered by having attractively waved petals. The most famous of these sports occurred in 1899 at Althorp, the country seat of the Earl Spencer, and was named 'Countess Spencer'. It was then crossed back to the huge range of grandifloras which Eckford and others had developed, giving rise to the whole race of 'Spencer' sweet peas. So popular did this new strain become that large areas in California were put down to seed production to satisfy the demand, and the National Sweet Pea Society was founded.

TOP TIP
Towards the end of summer, leave a few seed heads on annual plants as the seeds can be collected in the autumn for sowing the following spring.

PERENNIALS

Perennials are the mainstay of the summer flower border. They are the plants that cover the ground, add height and give volume and colour to the garden.

Shop regularly and in every season to give your garden interest all year round. A few plants bought in flower in spring, summer, autumn and even winter will immediately give seasonal interest to the garden. Build up a portfolio of perennials of different heights, foliage forms and shapes, buying taller plants for the back of a border and shorter ones for the front.

Must-have easy perennials for the summer garden

Hardy geraniums (*Geranium* spp.) are the ideal beginner's plant. Coming in all colours and varieties that grow in sun or shade, they are rarely bothered by pests, flower profusely and, if cut back after the flowers have faded, will often grow fresh foliage and produce more flowers.

Daisies (*Anthemis* spp.) are perfect summer flowers: they are rarely attacked by slugs and will flower for weeks on end.

Hattie's pin cushions (*Astrantia* spp.) are happy in sun but prefer dappled shade and moist soil. Pest and disease free, they will flower continuously over the summer and again if cut back to the ground after the first flowers have finished.

Verbascums (*Verbascum* spp.) have stately spires of flowers, adding vertical accents to borders. There are many varieties and all will flower for weeks and, once cut back after the first spire has finished, will continue flowering all summer.

Oriental poppies (*Papaver orientale*) have lush colours and flamboyant flowers from late spring. Flowering only once, they are worth it for their simple beauty. They never have trouble with pests and, once they have finished flowering, can be cut back hard – both foliage and flower spike – to the ground; new foliage will then follow.

Penstemons (*Penstemon* spp.) are a great choice for small gardens. They flower from May to September and should be cut back to 30 cm from the ground in mid spring to perform again.

Macedonian scabious (*Knautia macedonica*) is tough, great for dry soils in full sun and flowers its head off all summer, needing only to be dead-headed regularly to keep the plant at its peak performance.

SLUGS AND SNAILS
THE HORRIBLE TRUTH

Britain has the ideal climate for slugs and snails: our cool, damp summers and warmish, wet winters allow them to be active and breeding for most of the year. Hot, dry weather and cold, icy conditions kill them off.

THERE ARE ABOUT THIRTY different types of slug found in Britain, not all of which cause damage to plants. All have both male and female organs and, although they use either set of organs to cross-fertilize, can also fertilize themselves. They lay eggs about six times a year in clusters of around 80, which normally hatch within a few weeks, but can lie dormant until the right conditions occur. Each cubic metre of garden contains, on average, up to 200 slugs, and each slug has the potential to produce 90,000 grandchildren.

SLUGS have one large foot which secretes slime or mucus which is used for navigation, reproduction, self-defence and mating. It even enables them to travel over a sharp edge of glass without cutting themselves. A slug breathes through its skin, which must be moist in order to exchange gases. A slug's slime gathers moisture out of the air like a sponge on damp days and from the soil on dry ones. If the mucus dries out the slug will die, which is why ashes, soot, egg shells, sawdust and coffee grounds are all useful slug repellents — they draw the moisture from the slugs and disable them.

THERE ARE THREE COMMON TYPES OF SLUGS
in our gardens — the grey field slug, the garden slug and the black slug. **The grey field slug** is the most common and damaging. Up to 3.5 cm long, it relishes tender foliage and is typically found munching through hostas, lilies, petunias and dahlias, not to mention lettuces, cabbages, carrots, beans, celery and tomatoes — in fact almost every type of garden crop. It continues to be active and feed in temperatures as low as

freezing. **The garden slug** is another small slug. Usually black with a pale side stripe, it feeds both above and below the ground, attacking leaf and root crops and is a particular pest of potatoes. **The black slug** is the monster of all slugs, growing up to a whopping 20 cm long. It attacks seedlings in spring.

Dealing with slugs and snails

There's no escaping the fact that slugs enjoy the majority of plants in the garden — the emerging shoots of most plants seem to succumb to an overnight slug attack and it can be quite depressing to come out in the morning and witness the devastation. Damage limitation is the answer, however: there are some plants that slugs absolutely love, some they hate and others they will have if they are desperate.

The Love List	The Hate List
Hostas, delphiniums, irises, tulips, dahlias	Lavender, verbascum, rock rose, lamb's ears, sage

The Damage Limitation List

These are rarely attacked — slugs and snails may nibble and hide under their leaves, but they never completely destroy the plants: hardy geraniums, roses, ornamental onions, honeysuckle, astrantias, columbine and most plants with hairy leaves, such as oriental poppies, or aromatic leaves, such as herbs or even ornamental grasses.

SLUGS DON'T LIKE garlic or coffee grounds. They hate caffeine, as it causes them to produce an excess of slime which immediately dries them out and prevents them from moving onto and eating the plants. Spent coffee grounds spread around a line of emerging seedlings or a new plant will keep the slugs off.

The garlic method is also very effective and was given to *Gardeners' World* by Una Dunnett, a hosta fanatic. Boil two crushed cloves of garlic in just over a litre of water for 3 to 4 minutes. Strain the mixture and make it up to a generous litre again, as some water will have been lost during the boiling process. Decant into a bottle. Add one tablespoon of the garlic water to 4.5 litres of water in a watering can and wet the leaves of precious plants in the late afternoon on a dry day. The mixture will dry on the leaves and the slugs will leave them alone. Reapply after rain, as the garlic will have been washed off.

> **TOP TIP**
> *Slugs and snails often make a beeline for newly planted specimens, so concentrate your efforts on protecting these rather than every plant in your garden.*

GARDENING FOR WILDLIFE

Even if you live right in the middle of a city, if you plant a tree,
you'll attract an insect. If you attract an insect, you'll entice a bird.
The bird will want a mate and you're on your way. If you fill your
garden with as wide a diversity of plants as you can, you'll soon
be surrounded by literally millions of creatures.

GEOFF HAMILTON
Geoff Hamilton's Paradise Gardens

If you have flowers in your garden you will attract wildlife.
Whether you choose native or non-native plants, the bees,
butterflies and other insects will arrive regardless. The
trick is to provide a wide variety of plants from evergreens,
wildflowers, garden plants, annuals and fruit which will
provide a year-round food supply. Single flowers are better
than double ones in this respect as their design makes it
easier for insects to reach the nectar and pollen.

A GARDEN FOR WILDLIFE does not need to be untidy,
but letting flowering plants die off naturally and then tidying
up in winter is better than cutting them back in early autumn:
if you do this, you will deprive the birds of valuable food
sources such as the seed heads of plants like teasels.

TOP TIP
If you have a pond, place a few large rocks
near the edge for smaller birds, butterflies
and insects to land on.

WHY ARE SOME PLANTS SCENTED?

It all comes down to reproduction. Most flowering plants rely on insects to transfer their pollen so that seeds can be produced, and one way to attract insects is through smell — hence perfumed flowers. Insects such as butterflies are very sensitive to plant scents, and can find a perfumed flower from quite some distance.

Flowers have to put a lot of energy into producing perfume and produce most scent when the chances of their insect pollinators being around to smell it are best. That means that most flowers are most strongly perfumed on warm, sunny days, when there's not much wind — in other words, in conditions that allow the insect pollinators to be out and about. They also don't start producing their scent until they're fully opened and ready to be pollinated, so a half-opened bud won't have much scent. Once the flower has been pollinated it doesn't need to attract more insects, so again it will save its energy and stop producing perfume.

Some plants are pollinated by night-flying insects such as moths and release scent as evening approaches. Honeysuckle and tobacco plants are evening scented and manna for moths.

Scent is usually produced in the petals, the surface of which has a layer of epidermal cells where various types of fragrant, or essential oils, are made. The scent of each flower is chemically quite complex: for example, the clove scent of pinks is made up of about 60 different chemicals. All the while the flower is closed, the essential oil remains in storage in special cells. When the flower opens, the oil is activated: the chemicals form a vapour which hovers round the plant and which we smell as scent. Flowers with thick, waxy petals such as lily of the valley keep giving out perfume for longer than flowers with thin petals.

In general, the more colour the petals have, the less essential oil is produced. White flowers tend to smell the most strongly, followed by pale yellow, pale pink and mauve-pink.

WHAT PLANTS TO GROW

UMBELS ARE PLANTS whose flowers look like upside-down umbrellas. They are made from loads of tiny flowers and attract all sorts of insects to their landing stage to pollinate each flower. Wild flowers such as wild carrot and cow parsley are umbels, as are garden flowers such as astrantias and sea holly, and herbs such as fennel. All of them are good news for insects.

BEES NEED FOOD from very early in the year, so winter flowers like the lungwort (*Pulmonaria* spp.) are great for them and for the gardener. The bee balm (*Monarda* spp.) flowers later in the year and is covered in bees and other insects. In the same plant family oregano and sage are useful for the kitchen and invaluable for bees.

DAISIES ARE ESSENTIAL in wild and cultivated form because their centres contain an abundance of nectar. The centre of each flower is made up of multitudes of tiny flowers, all of which contain nectar, and their petals send a message to the insects to show them where to get it!

DON'T MAKE THE MISTAKE of thinking that all native plants are weedy and invasive. Many are perfectly well behaved: they support native insects and bring lots of beauty to the border. The meadow cranesbill (*Geranium pratense*), foxgloves (*Digitalis* spp.), Jacob's ladder (*Polemonium* spp.), bellflower (*Campanula* spp.) and meadow clary (*Salvia pratensis*) are all good additions to the garden.

SOME ROSES HAVE BEAUTIFUL HIPS if they are not dead-headed, and provide food for birds in the late autumn and early winter (see page 28).

WHEN PRIMROSES FLOWER IN SPRING, they produce nectar early in the year for insects, and later on finches are attracted to their seeds.

MARIGOLDS GIVE NECTAR FOR INSECTS and are a good choice if planted with vegetables — they make an attractive combination and will lure some insects away from your crops.

LAVENDER SMELLS GREAT and bees love the flowers, finches love the seeds.

HONEYSUCKLE HAS A POTENT FRAGRANCE and both birds and insects are drawn to the nectar. Later in the year the berries are an additional food source for birds and small mammals.

MICHAELMAS DAISIES AND *VERBENA BONARIENIS* flowers attract butterflies.

IVY PROVIDES NECTAR for insects and berries for the birds. It also offers shelter: blackbirds, robins and many other birds build their nests in its tangled branches.

AUTUMN

Now, though, the soft light of autumn brings out the warmth of
the garden again. It will rake and pull at shadows and illuminate
spent summer growth, colouring berries and leaves, teasing out
the best things in this season.

DAN PEARSON
The Garden

Autumn is about fiery oranges and yellows and the silvery
shimmer of ornamental grasses in flower. Deciduous plants
have reached their full potential and are having a final fling
before winter. It's a time for planting bulbs and hardy annuals
for spring and it's a great time for planting shrubs.

AUTUMN SHRUBS

What is a shrub and what makes it different from a tree? Trees
and shrubs all have one thing that distinguishes them from the
rest of the plant world and that is a woody stem that lives for
many years. Other plants may be perennial, but their tops
regrow year after year from rhizomes, bulbs or other organs
found at or just under the soil surface.

Trees and shrubs can be deciduous or evergreen. If a
plant's leaves stay green and alive through the winter it is called
an evergreen — holly and ivy are two of the best known examples
(see page 55). Plants whose leaves die in autumn and fall off,
such as oak, ash and horse chestnut, are called deciduous.

Though no scientific definition exists to separate trees and
shrubs, a general rule is that a tree is a woody plant with one
erect perennial stem — the trunk — at least 7.5 cm in diameter

at a point around 1.5 metres above the ground; a definitely formed crown of foliage; and a mature height of at least 4 metres. A shrub can therefore be defined as a woody plant with several perennial stems that may be erect or close to the ground. It will usually have a height of less than 4 metres and stems no more than about 7.5 cm thick.

THE REASON AUTUMN IS THE IDEAL TIME to plant shrubs is that the soil is still warm enough to encourage some root growth before the onset of winter, and the autumn rain ensures there is enough moisture for this to happen. Both these things help the shrub establish quickly so that it is more able to withstand any hot, dry spells the following summer.

> ### TOP TIP
> *When buying a shrub always consider the site*
> *where you want to plant it and look on the label*
> *to see whether it is suitable for sun or shade.*

PLANTING A SHRUB. Water the shrub thoroughly in its pot and put it to one side to drain. Then dig a hole at least twice as wide and deep as the shrub's container. Mix the removed soil with well-rotted organic matter and leave to one side. On heavy or chalky soils break up the sides and bottom of the hole by gently pricking the surfaces with a fork – this will allow the roots to grow into the surrounding soil.

Shrubs should be planted at the same depth as they were in the pot. Check that the hole is the right depth by standing the shrub (still in its pot) in the hole and laying a cane or piece of straight timber across the surface. If the shrub is standing too high or low, remove or add some soil in the bottom of the hole.

Lay the pot on its side and, with one hand supporting the shrub, ease the rootball out. Carefully tease out any roots that were circling around the bottom or sides of the pot so that they grow away from the rootball and into the surrounding soil. Position the shrub in the centre of the hole, then stand back to make sure that the best side is facing the front. When you are happy, fill in the gaps around the sides of the rootball with soil mixture, firming it down gently in layers as you work your way up to the top.

Once the hole has been filled, gently firm the soil once more to get rid of air pockets and make sure the plant is secure. Water the shrub again using at least one full watering can.

Then cover the surface of the soil with a generous layer of mulch to help prevent weeds growing and to reduce water loss from the soil. Autumn is normally a rainy season, but even so you should make sure that the shrub does not dry out in its first weeks of life in a garden border.

TOP TIP
Always consider the eventual height and spread of a tree or shrub when deciding where to plant it.

Failsafe shrubs for autumn colour

Guelder rose (*Viburnum opulus*) is an easy-to-grow 'native' shrub tolerant of most soils and situations. It has lovely orange and red leaves in autumn along with red berries.

Japanese maple (*Acer palmatum*). There are scores of varieties to choose from but the main reasons for growing any of them are their graceful shape and autumn colour. Most do well in pots but the most important thing to remember about acers is that they prefer dappled shade and must be kept out of the wind, as this will burn the leaves. 'Senkaki', 'Bloodgood' and 'Dissectum' are good ones to look out for.

Spindleberries (*Euonymus europaeus*) are not the most 'showy' of shrubs throughout the year, but in autumn their leaves turn a rich red and are covered in extraordinary red berries that open to reveal orange seeds.

Callicarpa bodinieri **'Profusion'.** Often needing a matching partner to produce berries, this shrub's leaves turn violet in the autumn and are accompanied by shiny, round, violet berries.

HARDWOOD CUTTINGS can be taken once the leaves have fallen from deciduous shrubs towards the end of autumn. Cut pencil-thick lengths of stems about 15–20 cm long, cutting just above a bud at the top and below a bud at the bottom. Make the cut above the bud a slanting one, as it is essential that the cutting is kept the right way up and this will differentiate it from the cut at the bottom.

Find a place in the garden that is out of direct sunlight but not in heavy shade and, using a spade, make a slit in the soil. If the soil is heavy, add a bit of sand to the bottom of the slit to help with drainage. Push the cuttings in, leaving the top half or a couple of buds sticking out of the soil. Close the slit, label, and water in dry weather. A year later the cuttings should have rooted and be ready to plant out or at least pot up.

Shrubs which make good cutting material

Dogwoods (*Cornus* spp.) are grown for their coloured stems which shine out in late autumn and throughout winter. Colours range from bright red to black and it makes sense to plant them in a group. They are easy to grow from cuttings, so one plant can be multiplied to produce the desired effect. Their bright stems look outstanding with snowdrops or spring bulbs and, in early spring, the stems can be cut to the ground and left to grow over the summer.

Buddleja **spp.** There is a huge variety of 'butterfly bushes' to choose from and they are an increasingly valuable plant for our butterfly population. For wildlife gardens they are essential. This is another shrub that benefits from cutting to 30 cm from the ground in early spring to keep it young and healthy.

Roses (*Rosa* spp.) can also be grown from cuttings and this can be a very economical way to increase a stock of good hedging varieties like *Rosa rugosa* or to renew an old but favourite plant that needs to be replaced. See Flowers, page 23, for more about roses.

──── OTHER FEATURES OF AUTUMN ────

One type of garden that really comes into its own in autumn is the prairie style. It's a bit like a very tall meadow which grows over the summer and reaches a peak of colour, height and form at this time of year. It's surprisingly easy to re-create a North American prairie in your back garden by mixing native American perennials such as daisies together with ornamental grasses. Most prairie plants like to be planted in sun, are tolerant of most soils and require little maintenance.

DAISIES ARE MAJOR CONTRIBUTORS to the
autumn and to the prairie garden. There are thousands of
varieties — about one in ten of the whole plant world belongs
to the daisy family — and there are a few that add a natural
feel to a prairie planting, as they will come to their peak of
performance at the same time as the grasses they are planted
alongside. Vibrant, long lasting, totally hardy and dying
gracefully, they also provide a huge quantity of nectar to
visiting insects. Rudbeckias (coneflower), heleniums
(sneezeweed), helianthus (perennial sunflowers), echinaceas
(purple coneflower) and asters (Michaelmas daisies) are all
incredibly easy to grow and need no pampering apart from
a little support and protection from slugs early in the year,
which is the best time to plant them, so that they can get
their roots down into the soil over the summer.

ORNAMENTAL GRASSES have become the ultimate
in low-maintenance planting and add grace, movement and
texture to any planting scheme. They need no cosseting and are
rarely attacked by pests such as slugs and snails. The only care
most of them need is a haircut in the spring. And there are lots
to choose from, varying in height from a mere 30 cm to over
1.8 metres, so they can be great ground cover or add statuesque
form to the border. Some of the tall ones flower in autumn,
when the low sun and early frosts add an extra dimension to
these fantastic plants.

Great garden grasses

Tall

Miscanthus sinensis 'Autumn Light'

Miscanthus 'Ferner Osten'

Miscanthus 'Kleine Fontane'

Calamagrostis 'Karl Foerster'

Calamagrostis 'Overdam'

Stipa gigantea

Mid height

Deschampsia 'Bronzeschleier'

Deschampsia cespitosa

Pennisetum 'Woodside'

Short

Anemanthele lessoniana

Stipa tenuissima

Carex testacea

Carex buchananii

DON'T CUT BACK GRASSES or prairie plants in the autumn because, in addition to being beautiful when they are covered in frost, most of them have seed heads which can be food for birds once they have finished flowering. Leave cutting back till the spring, but then you can be ruthless – cut them all right back to the ground.

AUTUMN IS THE PERFECT TIME to collect seeds. Harvest the seeds of hardy annuals, sweet peas and other favourites, then either store them over winter and sow them in spring or sow them in autumn for early summer flowers.

When the seed pod is ripe for harvesting it will become dry and usually change colour from green to brown or white; the seed itself will also change from green to brown, black or white. Always harvest your seeds on a dry day. Autumn days often start misty and dewy, so wait until the sun burns this off – around midday or early afternoon is the optimum time for seed collecting. The essential kit is a pair of scissors, paper envelopes and a pen. Simply cut off the seed head, place it into the envelope and write the name of the plant on it.

Most seeds will separate from their pods very easily if you just shake the envelope. Some seed pods, like those of the poppy, are like mini pepper pots and can simply be emptied out. Others are a bit sticky and may need to be cut open with a pair of scissors; still others are tough and have to be crushed with a rolling pin. If you do this on a clean sheet of paper, you can then either gently blow the chaff away, leaving the seed behind, or push it through tea strainers of various sizes until just the seed is left.

Seed needs to be absolutely dry before it is stored – damp seed will only rot. Leaving the seed in a dry environment for a couple of days is a good idea as this ensures that it dries out completely before you finally pack it in labelled paper envelopes. You can then store several envelopes in an old ice-cream carton or biscuit tin. The seed needs to be kept cool, dark and dry over the winter, so the fridge is an ideal place for it.

HYBRID SEEDS ARE OFTEN MENTIONED but rarely explained – this simply means that a plant has mixed parentage. Even if both the 'parent' plants are of one uniform colour and height, they will still carry genes for other heights and colours; they may also cross-fertilize with other plants of the same type grown in the garden. So their seeds will carry a mixture of those genes. If you collect and sow seeds from a hybrid they will sometimes produce plants like the original (this is known as 'coming true') but may produce plants of different colours and heights too.

F1 hybrids are produced when growers deliberately cross-pollinate two particular plants. They are the first generation of plants produced from the cross, and can only be produced by crossing the two particular parent plants again. As with other hybrids, seed saved from F1 plants will not 'come true'.

PLANTING BULBS

Plant spring-flowering bulbs from September onwards, so that they have time to produce new roots before the onset of winter. Tulips are the main exception to this rule – they can be planted in late autumn or even early winter without adversely affecting the flowering for the following season. Bulbs such as lilies and gladioli that flower in the summer are planted in the spring.

The more bulbs you plant, the better the garden will look in spring. Plant them in clumps of at least five, seven or nine. For the best and most natural effect, never plant bulbs in rows. Dig a hole three times the depth of the bulb and drop it into the bottom.

In their first year, bulbs are more or less guaranteed to flower no matter what, even if you don't plant them at the regulation depth. Plants are very clever and will pull themselves down to a depth where they are happy to grow eventually. However, it sometimes helps to plant them deeply as they are less likely to get sliced by errant spades or speared by forks later in the season when you have forgotten all about them. Most bulbs love good drainage, which means adding grit to the soil and a sunny spot.

PLANTING TIPS. Plant bulbs with the 'nose' (pointed bit where the shoot comes out) at the top and the 'basal plate' (flat bit where the roots are produced) at the bottom. To achieve a natural-looking swathe of bulbs in lawns or under trees, try grabbing a handful, throwing them on the ground and then planting them exactly where they land. With small bulbs, make a slit in the lawn with a knife, waggle the knife to make a small hole and then just drop the bulb in. Larger bulbs may need a trowel or a strong bulb planter. Hand bulb planters are really not strong enough for planting in lawns, but all right for planting in the border.

TOP TIP
*Most bulbs look best in informal
groups of odd numbers.*

MICE AND SQUIRRELS LOVE BULBS, so cover the area just planted with a layer of chicken wire to prevent them from being dug up and eaten.

PLANT BULBS IN POTS for instant spring impact, particularly if space is at a premium. If you plant an odd number to a pot and cover them with chicken wire, they can be growing on quietly over the winter and when they are just about to flower in the spring you can plant the whole pot in a border to give instant colour. Once the flowers have faded, take the pot out and allow the leaves to die down over the summer, to be brought out again the following spring.

PLANTS AND SEX

Until the eighteenth century Western people knew about birds but not bees. How did plants reproduce? How were seeds formed?

With the invention of the microscope in the early seventeenth century, scientists could observe minute phenomena invisible to the naked eye, and by the early eighteenth century naturalists were gradually starting to realize the shocking truth that plants had male and female organs.

Around 1720, Thomas Fairchild, working in a nursery in Hoxton in London, demonstrated the role of insects in plant reproduction. He showed that by transferring the pollen of a sweet William to the pistil of a carnation he could produce a hybrid with mixed characteristics. This became known as 'Fairchild's mule'. Although the Chinese had been doing this sort of thing for centuries before the West cottoned on, this was the first hybrid cultivated in Europe.

The outrage at Fairchild's interference with God's grand design was comparable to the current controversy over genetically modified plants, but his experiments led the way to a whole new method of developing plants. Previous plant innovations had depended on chance seedlings, the selection of good plants from cuttings or introductions from abroad. Fairchild bequeathed a sum of money to defray the expenses of an annual lecture which was to be held every Whit Tuesday forever on the subject of 'The Wisdom of God in the Vegetable Kingdom'. This lecture is still held and organized by the Worshipful Companie of Gardeners at St Giles at Cripplegate in London.

WHY DO LEAVES CHANGE COLOUR in the
autumn? Chlorophyll — which gives plants their green colour
— is not the only pigment in leaves. There are yellow and
orange ones too, but during spring and summer they are
usually masked by the green of the chlorophyll. With the onset
of shorter, cooler days in the autumn, trees start to prepare
for winter. Photosynthesis stops when it is cold and light levels
are low. The chlorophyll in the leaves breaks down and the
yellow and orange pigments begin to show through. One
of these, carotene, holds up much better under sunlight
than chlorophyll, so when chlorophyll disappears from leaves,
carotene is left behind. Since carotene absorbs blue-green
and blue light in sunlight, the light it reflects back to our
eyes from leaves is yellow.

So why are some leaves red? Another pigment called
anthocyanin is formed when sugars and certain proteins
interact in the sap inside plant cells. Although anthocyanins
play no part in photosynthesis, they are not formed unless
sunlight is present and, since they absorb blue, blue-green
and green light, the colour they reflect to our eyes is red.

The colour produced by anthocyanins is also sensitive
to the pH, or degree of acidity, in the cell sap. If the sap
is very acidic, anthocyanin imparts a bright red colour;
if the sap is less acidic, its colour is more purple.

WINTER

If you have a proportion of plants which remain in winter it helps
to keep the garden alive and if you can retain a few seed-heads
or attractive grasses they also help to create little scenes.

BETH CHATTO
Beth Chatto's Green Tapestry

Winter for the gardener seems to go on forever: there is no
real full-stop between autumn and winter, nor between winter
and spring. There are short, dark days and months when it
seems that there is nothing happening, but things certainly
are, it's just that they are mostly going on underground. Bulbs
and perennials, for example, are making roots and tiny shoots,
ready to erupt out of the ground once the temperatures are
right for them. The challenge for the gardener is to make
the winter garden as interesting as possible with occasional
flowers, powerful scent, and strong textures and form.

EVERGREENS

When everything else has died down or dropped its leaves,
the mainstays of the winter garden are the evergreens. As a rule
of thumb, to have a garden that holds its own during the winter
months, one third of the planting should be evergreens and
that can be anything from topiary, hedges and bamboos to
shrubs, trees and perennials.

TWO OF THE MOST enduringly popular evergreens are
the ones most closely associated with Christmas celebrations –
holly and ivy.

HOLLY (*Ilex* spp.) makes a really good specimen shrub or small tree; it is also a good topiary plant because it is slow-growing and its leaves grow closely together. There are plenty of elegant varieties to choose from and they thrive in dappled or full shade, tending to prefer well-drained soils and disliking extreme moisture or drought. Berries can come in a variety of colours from red or yellow to black but, unless the variety is self-pollinating, both male and female varieties need to be planted together.

The following hollies need another plant
with them in order to form berries:

Ilex aquifolium (**common holly**)
Ilex aquifolium '**Handsworth New Silver**'

These are self-fertile:
Ilex aquifolium '**J C van Tol**'
Ilex aquifolium '**Pyramidalis**'

Always look on the label for information
on male, female or self-pollinating varieties.

IVY (*Hedera helix*) is a woody evergreen climber which attaches itself to trees or walls by means of short stem roots. It has round clusters of green and yellow flowers in autumn and produces berries which ripen to become purplish-black by early spring. It is an important food plant for insects and birds, providing a late supply of nectar in autumn and berries during hard winters when food may be scarce. Ivy also provides good cover for nesting and roosting birds.

Easy evergreen shrubs

In addition to holly and ivy, try these for year-round interest.

Box (*Buxus sempervirens*) makes a perfect small hedge but, much better, can be clipped into topiary shapes (see page 146). What box needs is a once-yearly clip from June to September to keep it in shape.

Eleagnus x ebbingei is a bushy and dense shrub. Some varieties have yellow variegation that can light up a winter border. It's also good for winter fragrance.

Strawberry tree (*Arbutus unedo*) is a marvellous small tree or large shrub with wonderful bark texture, glossy leaves and bell-shaped flowers which appear in autumn and winter alongside the ripening strawberry-like fruits from the previous season.

Spindle (*Euonymus* spp.) is a very useful small shrub, good for ground cover under trees or shrubs or for growing on banks. There is a range of varieties with variegated gold or silver leaves which brighten up dull corners.

See Design, page 144, for more about evergreens. Yew, camellias, bamboo and viburnums are all easy to grow.

AS AN ALTERNATIVE TO EVERGREENS there are also the 'evergreys', which are simply evergreens with silver leaves. Santolina and lavender are two useful shrubs that keep their delicately coloured leaves during the winter and add structure and interest to the garden.

THE HOLLY AND THE IVY

The use of these two plants as seasonal decoration has crossed over from pagan to Christian tradition. They were once banned from Christian churches until a Christian emphasis was given to their use by likening the holly berries to the blood of Jesus and the prickles to the crown of thorns worn at the Crucifixion.

Holly was traditionally considered to be a masculine plant and ivy a feminine one. Although it was thought to be unlucky to bring ivy into the house at other times, it was allowed at Christmas, as a bringing together of male and female attributes in harmony. It is said that if you bring prickly-leaved holly into the house for Christmas the husband will rule the household for the coming year; if the holly is smooth-leaved it will be the wife who is in charge.

To pagans holly was a symbol of everlasting life, used in celebrating the winter solstice. It was also thought to keep away witches and evil spirits, and to give power over horses.

Ivy has been held in high esteem throughout recorded history. Priests in ancient Greece gave wreaths of ivy to newly married couples as an emblem of fidelity. Its leaves were used by the Romans for wreaths in depictions of Bacchus, the god of wine, to whom the plant was dedicated. It was thought that binding the brow with ivy, or drinking wine in which ivy leaves had been boiled, would prevent or cure intoxication. Goblets were even made from the wood in the hope of achieving this. In England 'ale-stakes' of ivy-covered poles were erected outside taverns as innkeepers vied to have the biggest advertisement for the quality of their ale.

In folklore ivy was believed to be a plant of protection, keeping away the devil and evil spirits and charming away warts. In the highlands and islands of Scotland it was used with rowan and honeysuckle to make a charm for keeping evil spirits away from milk- and butter-making in the dairy.

PLANTING FOR WINTER

Evergreen shrubs, like deciduous ones, should be planted
in the autumn, when the soil is still warm and moist, so that
the plant can get its roots established.

PLANT TREES AND HEDGES from November onwards
as long as the soil is not frozen or waterlogged. This is a good
time to buy bare-root plants. This is the cheapest, and often
best way to buy hedges and trees, because, as long as they are
planted well, once spring arrives the roots start to grow and
will establish far quicker than a container-grown tree.

'SAUCER PLANTING' is the perfect method for planting
bare-root trees, and also works for container-grown specimens,
whose roots should be teased out prior to planting. Instead of
digging a huge hole and adding muck, the idea is to dig a shallow,
saucer-shaped hole with a slight mound in the centre. The hole
should be wider than the roots of the tree to encourage them
to move out horizontally, which quickly gives the tree stability.

Position the plant on the mound and gently spread out
the roots. Add compost or leaf mould to the excavated soil and
return the mixture to the hole. Stake the tree with a short post
hammered into the ground at a 45-degree angle and secured
with a tree tie. The lower stake allows the tree to flex in the
wind and strengthen, but at the same time supports the roots.

TOP TIP

*Structure is the key to winter interest in the garden,
using walls, paths, hedges and architectural planting,
alongside colourful barks and scented flowers.*

BARK

*As the profusion of the past six months ebbs away and the cloak
of colour and vegetation recedes again, the landscape of the garden is
revealed in a new light. The underlying skeletons begin to poke through,
the stark burst of growth on the limes is bared against the sky, with
a burst of red shoots that gives warmth in the grey days.*

DAN PEARSON
The Garden

Bark becomes one of the visible elements of the garden in
winter and some shrubs and trees are worth growing for their
bark alone, introducing a new textural and sensory element.

Plants for bark

Dogwood (*Cornus* spp.). The colour of dogwood stems shines
out from late winter to early spring ranging from bright red
to black. See page 46 for advice on propagating them from
hardwood cuttings.

Flowering cherry (*Prunus serrula*) is covered with masses of small
white flowers in May and, once mature, the bark peels away to
reveal a polished dark red mahogany-like trunk. Totally tactile!

Paperbark maple (*Acer griseum*) does what it says — old orange-
brown bark peels away to show a cinnamon-coloured stem.

Himalayan birch (*Betula utilis* 'Jaquemontii'). On a dull
winter's day the bright white bark contrasts well with the winter
landscape. The trunk can be washed to make it even whiter.

Willow (*Salix* spp.). Some willow shrubs are invaluable for their coloured stems. Great plants for wet soils and the margins of ponds, they need to be cut down in spring to get the brightest stems the following winter. Good varieties are *Salix* 'Britzensis', with bright scarlet stems, and *S. vitellina*, with golden stems.

--- FLOWERS FOR WINTER ---

As a bonus, nature gives many of these exquisite but diminutive flowers the most intense and delicious perfume. The scent of even the smallest flower can be really powerful and hit you unexpectedly from the other side of the garden.

RACHEL DE THAME
Star Plants

Winter-flowering shrubs emit the most powerful of all scents and it is quite possible to fill a garden with scent on a winter's day. The flowers are small and insignificant, but at this time of year they have very little competition for the attention of pollinating insects and therefore no need to be big and brash in order to attract them — the scent does the job for them. Plant one or two shrubs in the parts of the garden you visit

most in winter, such as along the
path to the front door or even by
the dustbins. Put one in a hidden
corner, or under a window that
you sometimes leave open. Cut
flowering branches of the most
vigorous shrubs to bring into
the house.

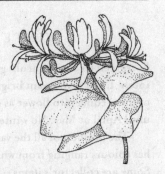

Plants for winter scent

Winter-flowering honeysuckle (*Lonicera purpusii/L. fragrantissima*)
is the perfect 'front garden' plant because when nothing else
is around the tiny flowers emit a sweet and powerful scent.
Cut stems to bring into the house for further enjoyment.

Wintersweet (*Chimonanthus praecox*) may take a while to get going,
but the perfume is worth waiting for. Place it where it can be
seen for winter enjoyment.

Christmas box or 'sweet box' (*Sarcococca confusa*) is a small,
evergreen shrub, covered with glossy green leaves and hardly
noticeable all year until the tiny flowers start to pump out
perfume in December. It's perfect for a pot by the door.

Witch hazel (*Hamamelis* spp.) has spidery flowers that open
on naked stems. For the best effect plant it in dappled shade
in a woodland setting. Try placing snowdrops under it for
a complete winter picture.

Daphnes (*Daphne* spp.) love a sunny spot and grow quietly
away all year before their tiny flowers appear in late winter.
They carry the perfume on into spring.

WINTER COLOUR

Evergreen trees and shrubs give the winter garden structural interest, but if you want bright colour, plant hellebores. Some of them come into flower as early as December and then persist until April or May. No winter garden should be without them.

The brashest of all the varieties is *Helleborus* x *hybridus,* which has colours ranging from white through to almost black. Some are collector's items — many gardeners travel miles to pick up precious colours from nurserymen. For something a little subtler, try *H. foetidus* (stinking hellebore) and *H. argutifolius* (Corsican hellebore), both with bright lime-green flowers.

HELLEBORES LIKE a soil that is rich in organic matter such as compost or leaf mould. It should be moist but not waterlogged; however, once they are established, they will cope with quite a bit of drought in the summer. They have a deep and extensive root system, so the planting hole should be much larger than the pot, to give them room to spread out. Hellebores will grow almost anywhere, but although they are often sold as shade plants they can struggle under deciduous trees where the tree roots take up most of the space.

CUT OFF THE LEAVES once the flowers appear, so that the flowering stems can be seen clearly. New leaves appear from the base at the same time as the flowers, so this is a good opportunity to tidy up the plants and add a mulch of compost to show them off to perfection.

HELLEBORES ARE VERY PROMISCUOUS and once one or two different colours are grown together they will produce loads of seed which you can either collect and sow in pots or leave to seed about in the garden. There is no guarantee that the colour of the flowers will be good, but it is worth the wait to see if something spectacular eventually emerges. This will require patience, as the seed can take 6–18 months to germinate and then another two or three years to flower, but it is a great way to increase plants in the garden for free and, more especially, to add winter interest.

IF YOU WANT TO GUARANTEE the colour of your flowers, divide hellebores at the same time as other herbaceous perennials – late spring or early autumn. Washing off excess soil helps you to see where it might be possible to divide the root system. Prise the plant apart and replant the new divisions, adding more compost and watering in well.

SNOWDROPS ARE BULBOUS plants and have a yearly growth cycle of which only a short period is above ground. In the wild they grow mostly in the woodland and forest regions of central and southern Europe, which experience definite seasonal climatic variations, namely cold winters and springs, warm dry summers and cool, often damp autumns. The snowdrop's life cycle is adapted to deal with these conditions. Once all top growth has disappeared – usually mid to late May – the plants enter a long dormant phase and stay underground, forming next year's flowers and leaves. When autumn arrives, and along with it the rain, the roots start to form and will slowly grow, stopping if the weather is too cold. In late winter or early spring the flower shoots emerge from the soil along with the leaves, and the cycle starts all over again.

SNOWDROP FOLKLORE

Snowdrops may not be native to Britain, even though they are seen growing in hedgerows and on the edge of woods. The first garden reference is in Gerard's *Herball* of 1597 and it is thought that monks may have brought snowdrops to Britain from Italy in the fifteenth century. Certainly they are often found in the gardens and churchyards of old monasteries, where they came to be associated with death and therefore viewed as bad luck. A single snowdrop blooming in the garden is supposed to be a sign of impending misfortune and, in the West Country, snowdrops cannot be brought into the house before the first chickens of the year are hatched.

'IN THE GREEN' is the term used for snowdrops lifted and divided after they have finished flowering. This is done when clumps become too large and don't flower well and, more particularly, to make more clumps. Snowdrops are often sold 'in the green' and this is the best way to buy them, as flowering is more or less guaranteed: a dry bulb may not be as successful.

DELICATE FLOWERS are all the more appreciated for their scarcity at this time of year, and among the bulbs and perennials the iris family have the most beautiful of all. Plant the bulbs of *Iris* 'Katherine Hodgkin' in shallow bowls or in sunny corners of the garden and watch them burst into flower in February, when there is hardly anything else coming out of the ground. *Iris unguicularis* is an extraordinary plant that flowers at any time from autumn to spring during mild spells – plant it against a wall so that it can benefit from any winter warmth. The exquisite lavender flowers, often hidden by the leaves, have delicate markings and are silky in texture. Pick them in bud before the slugs get them and take them indoors to unfurl for full appreciation.

CHAPTER TWO

FOOD

*If you were to ask me for my top kitchen-gardening
tip, I'd say that you'd do far better to grow half the
amount, but grow it twice as well.*

ALAN TITCHMARSH
The Kitchen Gardener

VEGETABLES

*It is hard to express in words the satisfaction that comes from having
a truly productive vegetable garden with no ground idle, no space
wasted and an abundance to pick for the kitchen.*

JOY LARKCOM
Grow Your Own Vegetables

THE EASIEST WAY TO GROW VEGETABLES is
in a raised bed. This saves on digging as, once the ground has
been properly prepared, it need not be walked on or dug again
for a considerable time.

IF YOU DON'T HAVE A RAISED BED, prepare the
ground thoroughly before planting anything in your kitchen
garden. Success with root vegetables in particular is very much
down to the quality of the soil they are grown in, so it's worth
taking the time to prepare your patch. Digging is an essential
task and fortunately it is the best way to keep warm on a winter's
day. It gets air into the soil to encourage bacterial activity;
exposes heavy soil to winter weathering and frost penetration,
which breaks it down; loosens compacted soil so that roots can
penetrate more deeply; and is a means of adding manure or
other organic matter to the soil.

DIGGING SHOULD ONLY BE DONE when the soil is
reasonably dry, never when it is wet enough to stick to the soles
of your boots. More harm than good can be done because the
soil becomes compacted, which ruins its structure and defeats
the whole object of digging.

There is an art to digging properly and it's quite simple.
Hold the spade upright and chop the blade into the ground

vertically. This puts less strain on the back and takes up the most soil with the least effort. Bend the knees and not the back when digging.

GARDENERS TALK A LOT about single-spit and double digging. A spit is a spade's depth of soil, about 23–25 cm. **Single-spit digging** means turning over the top layer of soil and adding manure or compost. Dig a trench to the depth of a spade and about 30 cm wide along the length of the area to be dug. Remove the soil to the end where the digging will finish. Add manure or compost to the bottom of the trench and then dig another trench parallel to the first, throwing the soil forward over the manure. In other words, use the soil from the second trench to fill in the first. Repeat this until you have dug over the entire area, then use the soil from the first trench to fill in the last. **Double-spit digging** is almost exactly the same as single digging, except that you fork the manure into the bottom of the trench to the depth of another spit before throwing the soil from the next trench on top. Although it is harder work, the benefits can last for up to three years, especially if soil has been compacted at the lower level. Roots penetrate deeper and extract water from the lower levels rather than depleting water from the upper soil level.

TOP TIP

A scaffold board is a useful piece of vegetable-growing kit. You can stand on it for planting so the soil surface is never compacted, it can be used as a straight edge for marking a line for sowing seeds and it acts as the perfect spacer between rows of vegetables.

THE COMPOST HEAP

*The compost heap is the manifestation of the principle of organics,
recycling waste and returning it to the soil to enrich future plant
growth, which in turn will provide for future compost.*

MONTY DON
The Complete Gardener

A compost heap is a pile of garden and kitchen waste such as
grass clippings and vegetable peelings. When heaped together,
these ingredients generate heat and decompose naturally with
the help of bacteria and fungi. In a good heap temperatures
can reach 60–70°C, which kills most weed seeds.

SOIL IS MAGIC

There are billions to hundreds of billions of micro-organisms
in a handful of typical garden soil. That single handful might
contain thousands of different species of bacteria, hundreds of
species of fungi and protozoa, dozens of species of nematodes
plus an assortment of mites and other micro-arthropods.
Almost all of these countless organisms are not only beneficial,
but essential to the life-giving properties of soil. If you dug up
a spadesful of soil it would have more species of organisms than
can be found in the entire Amazon rainforest above ground.

TOP TIP
*Compost is ready for use on the garden when it smells
pleasant, is blackish brown, moist and crumbly,
and has no large recognizable bits of vegetation in it.*

THE SECRET OF GOOD COMPOST lies in the ingredients. They need to be two-thirds from carbon sources and one-third from nitrogen sources. The carbon comes from woody prunings, the nitrogen from grass cuttings and kitchen waste. Where the balance of potential compost ingredients is in favour of the nitrogen sources, as it is in most households, then the perfect ingredients to redress this are scrunched up newspaper and cardboard, which also helps with recycling.

WHAT TO USE: Vegetable peelings, egg shells, tea leaves, tea bags, shredded paper and cardboard, garden waste, shredded stems of large plants, spent potting compost, grass clippings, annual weeds that haven't gone to seed and old bedding plants.

WHAT NOT TO USE: Diseased or pest-ridden plants; perennial weeds such as dock, couch grass, bindweed, and ground elder; big woody stems unless you shred them beforehand; meat, dairy or fat scraps from the kitchen; dog, cat or human faeces.

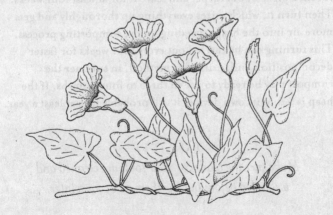

THE PERFECT
COMPOSTING METHOD

THREE BINS ARE IDEAL because you can be filling
one while the second is decomposing and you can transfer
the contents of the decomposing one into the third bin,
turning it as you go. However, most people don't have space
for that and it is better to have one bin than none at all. The
method is the same whether you use one, two or three bins.
Add suitable materials to the bin until it is full, then cover
it with a piece of old carpet and leave it for at least four weeks.
Then turn it, which mixes everything up thoroughly and gets
more air into the heap, speeding up the composting process.
This turning can be carried out every four weeks for faster
decomposition and, using this method, in summer the
compost may be ready to use in three to four months. If the
heap is left to its own devices it will probably take at least a year.

ESSENTIAL TOOLS

Always buy the best you can afford, because good tools will last a lifetime. A spade, fork, rake, hoe, trowel and watering can are the essential starter kit for growing vegetables and the best quality are usually made of stainless steel. There are various sizes of spade and fork – buy the one that feels the most comfortable.

Spades have been around for a long time, and the medieval version was either one- or two-sided, made from a single piece of straight-grained wood with a T-shaped handle added. It was shoed with iron nailed on at the sides. The mattock was used for hoeing, breaking up soil, digging trenches and rooting up unwanted shrubs and roots. The billhook was for pruning, making and laying hedges, coppicing and any other wood jobs – the term 'by hook or by crook' refers to the billhook. The sickle was used for cutting crops and trimming grass around tree trunks. The scythe was for mowing and cutting down the meadows. Forks and rakes collected dung and turned hay. Weeding was done with a weeding hook and forked stick.

The first trowel appeared in the middle of the seventeenth century in a book called *Elysium Britannicum* by John Evelyn. It looks a bit like a cement trowel and the design remained much the same until the 1830s, when the trowel took on more the form of a miniature spade.

The wheelbarrow first appears in western Europe in a stained-glass window at Chartres Cathedral dated 1220, but it was invented in China about 200 AD by Chuko Liang, who used it to transport supplies to his army over muddy soil and hilly terrain. The wheelbarrow was a labour-saving device and, on medieval building sites, it could do the work of two labourers for the price of one.

SEEDS

A seed contains everything it needs to grow into an entire plant and all the gardener has to do is to give it the right conditions. It is made up of three parts:

Embryo
A miniature plant in an arrested state of development.
It will begin to grow when conditions are favourable.

Endosperm
A built-in food supply, which can be made up
of proteins, carbohydrates or fats.

Seed coat
A hard outer covering, which protects the seed from disease and insects. It also prevents water from entering the seed and initiating germination before the proper time.

GERMINATION is a complex process whereby a seed embryo goes from a dormant state to an active, growing state. Before any visible signs of germination appear, the seed must absorb water through its seed coat. It also must have enough oxygen and a favourable temperature.

> ### TOP TIP
> *Soaking seeds with hard coats overnight before you sow them sometimes helps them to germinate a bit quicker. The smaller the seed the shallower it should be sowed.*

TOP TIP

Very small seeds can be mixed with a bit of sand before sowing. This is not only economical but stops them being sown too thickly.

SOWING VEGETABLE SEEDS outdoors is virtually the same as growing annuals (see page 29); the soil needs to be like fine breadcrumbs and warm enough. Seeds germinate at different soil temperatures, but rarely below 5°C. Almost all vegetable seeds germinate much faster in warm soils than in cold ones, so it is always best to wait before sowing them. It is possible to warm up the soil first by covering with clear polythene or cloches, but this only gives about two weeks' advance germination and most plants will catch up if they are sown late.

SOW THINLY. It is a waste to do otherwise. Seed sown too thickly will have to be thinned anyway and, for most crops, it is best to sow little and often to stagger the harvest. Always keep some seed back in case the first sowing fails. Use either a line of string attached to pegs or the side of a scaffold board to mark out a planting row. With a trowel, hoe, pointed stick or finger, draw a shallow line (or 'drill'), which can be from 1 to 5 cm deep depending on the size of the seed: seeds need to be covered by about twice their depth of soil. Put a few seeds in the palm of your hand, pinch a few between the other forefinger and thumb and drop them along the drill, spacing them as evenly as possible. Cover with soil, water gently and label the row.

ON DRY SUNNY DAYS it often helps to water the drill before sowing the seeds to help with water retention and, on dry, sandy soils, it is best to do this routinely. It is not necessary to water the drill afterwards if this method is used.

THINNING OUT SEEDLINGS may seem wasteful, but seeds will not develop properly if they are overcrowded. Thinning is easiest in moist soil, so if it is dry, water the seedlings an hour or so beforehand or in the evening on hot days. Choose weaker-looking seedlings if there are any and pull the stems out at ground level; for the first thinning, leave a gap of about 5 cm between the remaining seedlings, then firm them in.

Thin again once these have grown until the spacings are adequate: the distances will be different for each vegetable. For instance, a carrot may need to be 4 cm from its neighbour on either side whereas some varieties of lettuce may eventually need 30 cm. Read the seed packet for guidance.

KEEP CROPS COMING by sowing a row of vegetables every couple of weeks. The best time to sow is when the first row of the same variety is above ground and is at the thinning stage.

TOP TIP
Save space by sowing two different crops in a single row. Mix a slow-growing crop such as parsnips or carrots with something faster such as lettuces and radishes.

PLANTING BY THE PHASES OF THE MOON

'The moone in the wane, gather fruit for the last,
but winter fruite gather, when Mighel is past...'

Planting by the phases of the moon is enjoying a resurgence of
popularity and the basic principle is that the moon has gravity
which is felt on Earth. During the first half of the lunar month,
the moon grows from new to full and its gravitational pull upon
the ground beneath the gardener's feet increases. During the
second half of the month the moon wanes and its gravitational
pull decreases. In response, the water table, which is beneath
the Earth's surface no matter where in the world gardeners tend
their gardens and farmers farm their land, is drawn up and then
permitted to drop back, exerting increasing and then decreasing
upward pressure.

This monthly phenomenon creates unique conditions in
the garden's topsoil. From new moon to full moon, the moisture
in the Earth's crust moves upwards under the pressure that is
exerted by the rising water table, making more moisture available
within the top soil. This benefits any seeds sown and plants
put in the ground at that time. Additionally, the same upward
pressure encourages enhanced moisture absorption by seed and
plant, increasing the possibility of germination and plant survival.
From full moon to the next new moon, the pressure upon root
systems exerted by the prevailing moisture reduces as the water
table falls. This is the ideal time to prune, for example, because
the reduced pressure causes cut branches to bleed less.

CROP ROTATION

All vegetables have specific soil and mineral requirements, so grouping together crops with similar needs and planting them in a different place each year minimizes the build-up of pests and diseases and enables the soil to replenish its lost minerals.

THE THREE-YEAR ROTATION SYSTEM: Divide the vegetable garden into three plots and the crops into three groups, and plant a different group in each plot each year.

Brassicas including root brassicas	Other roots, solanaceae and alliums	Legumes
cabbages, broccoli, cauliflower, kale, turnips, swedes	potatoes, tomatoes, aubergines, peppers, carrots, beetroot, parsnips, onions, leeks, garlic	broad beans, peas, French and runner beans

LEGUMES LEAVE NITROGEN IN THE SOIL, which will help the leaves of brassicas to grow, so plant brassicas in last year's legume patch. Brassicas are hungry crops, drawing a lot of nutrients out of the soil; once they have gone, add manure to the patch where they have been, then plant the roots there and put legumes where the roots were. Common sense is the watchword — for instance, carrots and parsnips do not like heavily manured soil, so plant them elsewhere.

In small vegetable plots it is often not possible to follow rotation to the letter and, as long as the same crop is not grown in the same space every year (which would allow a build-up of pests and diseases), most vegetables will be happy.

QUICK-GROWING CROPS such as lettuces and
radishes can be fitted in where there is space, and tomatoes
and squashes can be grown with the legumes. If you have
room for a fourth bed, you can grow perennial crops such
as asparagus and rhubarb.

CARROTS

*With well-worked soil, proper thinning and regular watering, you
can enjoy crunchy carrots with flavours that are far more sweet and
satisfying than any carrot you can purchase at the supermarket.*

FERN MARSHALL BRADLEY & JANE COURTIER
The Complete Vegetable Gardener

Carrots like loose, sandy soil where their tap roots can get
down deep without hitting stones. If your soil is heavy or stony,
it is quite easy to grow carrots in containers filled with multi-
purpose compost. They don't like richly manured soil either.
One week before sowing your seeds, rake in a light dressing
of general fertilizer and that will be plenty.

CARROTS SHOULD BE SOWN VERY THINLY
because when they are thinned out the smell attracts the carrot

fly, which lays its eggs in the soil near the roots. Carrot fly is drawn by the smell of crushed foliage so, if you have to thin, reduce the risk of an attack by doing it in the evening on a still day, removing any thinnings and watering afterwards. Growing onions with carrots can help to disguise the smell, as can putting up a barrier. To be effective this needs to be at least 45 cm high, as the carrot fly travels close to the ground.

Keep the plants well watered during their growth period — too little water results in coarse, woody roots. It's best to harvest carrots in the evening, again to avoid attracting carrot fly.

HISTORY OF THE CARROT

The wild carrot can be found in Britain's countryside but the cultivated version didn't reach our kitchens until the sixteenth century: Flemish refugees brought it during the reign of Elizabeth I. By that time it had been cultivated for many centuries, though perhaps in a surprising form: in Roman times carrots were purple or white. Moorish invaders are thought to have brought purple and yellow varieties from North Africa to southern Europe around the twelfth century, and by the fourteenth century black, red and green/yellow carrots were also grown. The species did not turn orange until the 1500s when Dutch growers used a mutant seed from North Africa to develop a carrot in the colour of the House of Orange, the Dutch royal family.

ONIONS

Onions are as central a component of the vegetable garden as daffodils are to spring. You have to deliberately eschew onions for them not to be at the heart of the garden.

MONTY DON
The Complete Gardener

Onions – and their relatives – need a rich soil, plenty of water, sunshine and no competition from weeds. Give them these conditions and they are one of the easiest vegetables to grow. They can be grown from seed early in the year, but need a greenhouse or warm window-sill for a few weeks before they are ready to plant out. Far better, quicker and easier to buy onion sets, which come in bags and look like little onions, and get them into the ground as soon as it is warm enough in early spring. This also applies to shallots.

PUSH THE LITTLE ONIONS into well-prepared ground so that they are two-thirds buried and their noses stick out of the soil. During the next few weeks they will produce leaves and roots.

As with all bulbs, the leaves are the source of food which the plant needs in order to swell the bulb to a good size. When the leaves start to die back and before the plant produces flowers is the ideal time to harvest onions. Let the leaves die naturally and then lift the onions with a fork, leaving them on the surface of the soil to dry or take them under cover into a greenhouse. The drier they are the longer they will store.

SPRING ONIONS are fast-growing small onions that are grown from seed, harvested and eaten fresh as required.

Sow thinly in drills, then as they grow thin them to about 2 cm apart and use thinnings in the kitchen.

HISTORY OF ONIONS

Onions probably originated in central Asia – the first record comes from Babylon – but it was the ancient Egyptians who saw the bulb as a symbol of the universe and sacred to the goddess Isis. Commonly used in mummification and to repel snakes, it was also reputedly acceptable as currency. The *Ebers' Papyrus* of 1550 BC contains over 700 medicinal uses for onion, from healing insect bites to curing rabies. Ancient Greeks used onions to destroy warts and corns and also believed they were good for eyes and ears, the flow of urine, loosening mucus which rattled in the throat, and easing the bronchial symptoms of children and old people. It was the Romans who brought onions to England, along with leeks (which, like onions, belong to the *Allium* family) and many other vegetables.

GARLIC

There are two types of garlic, softneck and hardneck, though there is no difference in taste. If the stem at the top of the bulb is soft and papery, it is a softneck. Softnecks tend to have longer shelf lives than the hardnecks. They also tend to have more, but smaller, cloves per bulb, and are harder to peel. Hardneck garlic, as the name implies, has a hard stalk almost as thick as a pencil and develops an impressive flowering stalk, called a scape, which can grow 60–120 cm in height. The scapes on rocamboles, a relative of garlic, form beautiful circular curls and are prized by floral arrangers in some countries, especially Japan.

TOP TIP

*Cheat the root system to grow as late as February,
by half filling a cardboard toilet-roll tube
with damp compost and setting a clove on top.
Stand the tubes on a window-sill on damp
kitchen roll for a couple of weeks. Once roots
emerge from the bottom of the tube, plant
the clove outside, still within its tube, as soon
as the soil is warm enough.*

GARLIC NEEDS FULL SUN and a soil that will not
become waterlogged. Plant in late October or early November,
to give it time to form a good root system before the winter.
It will then stand at least 10°C of frost before rocketing into
growth in spring. Plant individual cloves just below the soil
surface 15 cm apart and in rows 30 cm apart.

GARLIC NEEDS AT LEAST A MONTH in soil
which is constantly below 10°C once its roots have developed
or it will probably not form cloves. If cloves don't develop,
lift the single bulb in July or August, dry it off and replant
in October. It will form extra-large heads (and cloves) in
the following summer.

IN THE GROWING SEASON it is important to nip
off flower buds as soon as they form as all the food and energy
must go into the bulb. Not all varieties routinely flower,
though. Sometimes 'top sets' or garlic cloves form on the
stalk. This is due to changeable weather in spring. Gather
and use the top sets in the kitchen.

HARVEST GARLIC once the leaves have started to fade and turn yellow by carefully lifting the bulbs with a fork. Remove any excess soil from the hairy roots, then lay the bulbs out to dry in an airy place. When they are 'rustling dry' they can be stored in ventilated containers until you're ready to use them. Some varieties will keep for a good ten months.

DON'T TRY TO PROPAGATE your own garlic. By nature it becomes progressively more diseased when growing in the soil — it is a race against time to harvest it before this affects the taste. Propagating your own is a recipe for bad crops next year and for introducing disease into your soil. It is also not advisable to plant cloves bought from a supermarket, as they may carry disease or virus and may not be suited to our climate. Instead buy them from a garden centre or mail-order supplier.

ELEPHANT GARLIC is six times the size of normal garlic, but occupies the same amount of growing space. The huge bulbs, each containing several cloves which can individually

THE MEDICINAL PROPERTIES OF GARLIC

The sulfides in garlic, onions and other members of the *Allium* family decrease the tendency for blood clots to form, which in turn lowers the risk of heart attacks and stroke; they may help to prevent hardening of the aorta, the major artery that carries blood from the heart; they lower the levels of low-density lipoprotein (LDL or bad cholesterol) and decrease total cholesterol; and they block the action of hormones or chemical pathways within the body that promote cancer.

Garlic also has a long folk tradition as an insect repellent used to combat aphids, white flies, spiders and other pests, but these traditions are rooted in science. In studies, garlic has successfully destroyed mosquito larvae and certain species of ticks, and has repelled mosquitoes, black flies, fruit flies and fleas. It can be used to prevent the spread of mould and repel insects from stored fruit, and some people even place garlic in drawers to repel moths. Garlic has also demonstrated success in repelling larger pests, including rabbits, moles and deer.

Further studies have found that garlic is effective as an insect repellent for humans when consumed or used as a spray. When garlic is eaten and its components are metabolized, compounds are released from the body through the skin and breath which can help ward off bugs.

be the size of regular garlic bulbs, are famous for their rich but milder flavour. The largest bulbs can reach a weight of 250 g or more and their tall flowering stalks can grow to a height of 1.5 metres, with a beautiful purple flower at the top. Elephant garlic (*Allium ampeloprasum*) is not a true garlic (*Allium sativum*), but is closer to the leek to which it bears a close resemblance in flavour. It is perfect for roasting as it does not fall apart in the oven.

GOURDS

Pumpkins and squashes are big, trailing plants that need lots
of room and really rich soil that hold plenty of moisture in summer.
A lot of people plant them on top of the compost heap so they can
feed off the rich, moist contents and scramble down over the sides,
where they don't take up much room.

ALAN TITCHMARSH
The Gardener's Year

Pumpkins, squashes, courgettes and marrows all need lots
of space, lots of rich soil and lots of moisture and will be
very happy growing on top of an old compost heap where
the heat and extra nutrition will make sure they romp away.

SOW THE SEEDS on their side with the pointed end
downwards and not too early, as they hate the cold: sow
indoors in pots in May and plant out in June, or sow
directly into the soil at the start of June. Cover each seed
with a cut-off lemonade bottle to provide added heat
and protection.

TOP TIP

To save space, train the trailing stems of squashes in circles
and pin the stems down with tent pegs to keep them in place.

ALL THE GOURDS ARE HEAVY FEEDERS: they
need a soil that is rich in organic matter and slightly acidic
(a pH of 5.8 to 6.8 is ideal). They also benefit from deep,
consistent watering, especially when the plants are in flower
and later when the fruits have started to swell. Mulch to lock

WHERE DO GOURDS COME FROM?

Pumpkins, courgettes and many other members of the squash family originate in Central America and have been used by indigenous people there for thousands of years. The earliest squashes were probably very small and bitter, and may have been used just for their edible seeds. Some tribes used squashes for making bowls and spoons, probably long before they used them for food.

The cucumber originated in the foothills of the eastern Himalayas, but was known to the ancient Romans: it was a favourite of the emperor Tiberius, whose gardeners created fantastic shapes by encasing cucumbers in wood, wicker or clay casks. Tiberius expected to be able to eat cucumbers at any time of the year, so his gardeners invented a system of growing them in portable beds: if cold weather was expected the beds could be wheeled indoors and sheltered behind windows of mica, a translucent stone.

George Stephenson, the great railway engineer, was also a keen gardener. He devised a system for growing straight cucumbers, using several glass cylinders made at his Newcastle steam engine factory. The growing cucumbers were inserted into the cylinders, which forced them to grow straight.

in moisture. On sandy or light soil, regular drenches with a liquid feed will help boost production.

HARVEST PUMPKINS AND WINTER SQUASHES in October when their skins have hardened and leave a little bit of the stalk on the top to prevent any rot getting in. The more sunshine they get the longer they will keep, so towards the end of September it is worth taking off a lot of the leaves and exposing the fruit to the sun for ten days so that they can ripen before harvesting. Most pumpkins will keep for a couple of months in cool, dark and dry conditions and some winter squashes will store for a lot longer.

COURGETTES WILL TURN INTO MARROWS if they are not picked young, and one plant is sufficient to feed a whole family with courgettes from early summer to the first frosts of autumn. To keep plants productive harvest courgettes about three times a week at the height of the season.

CUCUMBERS like the same growing conditions except that they need to have at least 100 frost-free days to mature. The hardy 'ridge' cucumbers are the best bet if no greenhouse is available and you have to grow them outside.

LEGUMES

The legume family of plants is the third largest in the world. Its members include beans, peas and lentils.

BEANS

There is a peculiar delight in eating peas that you yourself picked and potatoes that you have yourself dug. A garden is only half a garden that is limited to the cultivation of flowers, just as a life is only half a life that is limited to the cultivation of the aesthetic.

SPB MAIS

Runner bean seeds are twice as rich in protein as grains and well stocked in B vitamins and iron, whilst the green pods are high in vitamins A and C. Though generally grown as an annual in Britain, the runner bean is in fact perennial in its natural habitat of cool, shady valleys amid a mix of oak and pine forests. In the wild it is usually found at high altitudes and can survive at up to 2800 metres. The scarlet flowers attract hummingbirds and bees as pollinators.

There are two basic kinds of beans: bush beans that grow only a metre or so tall, and climbing beans that grow vines up to 3–4 metres long. The original beans that European explorers found in South and Central America were all climbers, but today there are more bush beans than climbing beans because people have bred the plants to stay short for the convenience of growing and harvesting.

IT IS A MISTAKE TO GROW row upon row of beans unless it is for the freezer: you will be inundated by them for a short period in summer. In small gardens beans can be grown up attractive wigwams or obelisks, alongside sweet peas. Both need picking regularly and the addition of decorative flowers means that more bees are attracted to pollinate the beans.

BEANS NEED LOTS OF MANURE AND MOISTURE and this means digging out a spit's depth of soil, adding manure and then covering it with the removed soil. Putting

---

TOP TIP

Some cultivars of French and runner beans produce coloured pods, which makes them useful in the ornamental garden. Good choices include 'Kingston Gold' (yellow) and 'Purple Teepee' (dark purple).

WHERE DO BEANS COME FROM?

Beans originated in Central and South America and were first farmed in Mexico more than 2000 years ago. There are over 4000 different kinds of beans in North America today, but only about one sixth of them are available commercially. The rest are in private collections and gene banks.

The scarlet-flowered runner bean arrived in Britain during the 1600s, having been collected in Virginia by John Tradescant and given to Charles I. It was initially grown as an ornamental plant – it was not until the 1700s that Philip Miller, who ran the Chelsea Physic Garden in London, advocated cooking and eating the green pods.

cardboard and shredded newspaper in the bottom of the trench also helps with moisture retention. A wigwam of strong poles like bamboo or hazel can then be built over the newly manured soil.

BEANS CAN BE STARTED OFF into growth indoors and grown on a window-sill but, like tomatoes (see page 100), they need to be hardened off before they are planted out. Where window-sill space is at a premium, sowing direct will be just as effective: push seeds into the soil alongside the wigwam support at the beginning of May. Plant two or three seeds as insurance against slugs and, for added protection, use a lemonade bottle cut in half and placed over the seed. This not only means the slugs won't get the seedlings, but it will also act like a small greenhouse.

TYING IN. Beans do twine, but not until they have reached a height of about 1 metre. Tie them in to the supports to get them going.

HARVEST REGULARLY and beans will keep on producing more. The more you pick the more you get and they will keep on going until the first frost kills them.

CLIMBING FRENCH BEANS are grown in exactly the same way as runner beans, and are just as tender and often tastier. They are ideal candidates for growing up supports in large pots and can make attractive plants in their own right. They are also self-pollinating, so are more likely to succeed in setting beans if weather conditions are not favourable for bees.

The Three Sisters — corn, beans and squash

Corn, beans and squash have been planted together by many indigenous people over many centuries. Historically, in many tribes the men cleared and prepared the land and then left their villages to hunt. The women planted corn and beans in mounds. The beans were a climbing variety, so they were able to use the tall corn stems for support. In return, the beans provided nitrogen for the corn. Beans have an unusual ability to draw nitrogen from the air and put it in the soil, and corn needs a lot of nitrogen to grow well. It's a great companionship.

Squash was grown in the space between the mounds, and as its long vines and large leaves covered the ground, it helped to prevent weeds from growing there. These three plants have such a harmonious relationship that they have long been called *the three sisters*.

PEAS

Peas come in two varieties: shelling and mangetout. Shelling peas mature at different times: earlies take around 12 weeks, second earlies 14 weeks and maincrops 16 weeks. They also come in round- and wrinkle-seeded varieties. Choose round seeds for hardiness and early sowing, and wrinkled for sweetness and summer sowings.

PEAS SOWN IN COLD, WET GROUND will rot, so make sure the soil is warm. They also love rich soil, so dig in compost prior to planting.

To grow an early crop, try sowing seeds in a length of old guttering. Drill drainage holes at regular intervals along the base. Fill to the top with seed compost and add an early pea variety, such as 'Feltham First', spacing the seeds about 7.5 cm apart. Place the guttering in a greenhouse or cold frame. Keep the compost moist and transplant into the garden once the seedlings have established. Dig out a shallow trench and gently slide the pea seedlings into it. Water and cover with cloches to encourage growth.

Regular picking is essential for a truly fresh pea. Harvest from the bottom of the plant and work upwards.

Do not pull the plant up after harvesting, as the roots are full of nitrogen-fixing bacteria, which will enrich the soil. Cut off the stems at ground level and allow the roots to rot down.

PEAS AND GENETICS

The science of genetics was invented by a nineteenth-century monk who enjoyed gardening. Gregor Mendel was abbot of the Augustinian monastery at Brünn (Brno) in what is now the Czech Republic, where he spent much of his time in the large gardens.

Mendel noticed that peas had certain characteristics that seemed to be passed from generation to generation. For example, plants with peas that were green had offspring with green peas, while those with yellow peas produced yellow offspring. Over seven years, Mendel carried out experiments with these plants, studying characteristics such as height, seed shape, seed colour and flower colour.

The experiments relied on studying pairs of characteristics that seemed to be 'either-or' in the plants. For example, the garden had tall pea plants and short pea plants, but no in-between ones. Mendel decided to cross a tall plant with a short plant and measure the result. To his surprise, all the offspring were tall, rather than the intermediate size that might have been expected. Continuing the experiment, he crossed the new tall plants with each other. In the next generation, three-quarters of the plants were tall, but one-quarter were short.

By observing that tall plants still had the potential to produce short offspring every now and again, Mendel had hit upon the concept of the recessive gene. Despite knowing nothing about DNA or the biochemistry of inheritance, he developed his two 'laws of heredity', which remain the basis of modern genetics.

MANGETOUT PEAS have exactly the same cultivation requirements as shelling peas except that they are harvested at the 'pod' stage, before the peas inside start to swell. Look out for seeds called 'Sugar Snap' or 'Purple Podded' for the best mangetout.

LETTUCE

There are four basic types: cos (also called romaine), leaf (also called loose-leaf), crisphead and butterhead. Their tastes vary a great deal, so the best lettuce to grow is the one that you will enjoy eating. Many of them are ideally suited to our climate – they dislike hot conditions and they need lots of rain. They also need rich soil.

LETTUCE SEEDS NEED TEMPERATURES below 20°C to germinate, so the key to success is to site them in a position which avoids the full blast of the sun in the middle of the day. Drying out often causes them to go to seed ('bolt') very quickly, though some varieties are more resistant to bolting than others.

FOR SMALL PLOTS, the 'cut and come again' varieties are the most useful: you harvest the leaves when you need them and the plants continue growing and providing fresh leaves. There are 'cut and come again' varieties of little gem, cos and butterhead lettuces.

REMOVE HARVESTED LETTUCES from the ground completely. If you leave the stump in the ground, it will rot and attract the attention of pests, root aphid in particular.

TOP TIP
For stir-fry leaves, try sowing some oriental greens. They will be ready for a 'cut and come again' harvest within weeks.

POTATOES

First earlies, second earlies and maincrop are categories of
potato which indicate when they can be harvested. First earlies
are usually harvested from June to July and eaten straight away.
Second earlies can be stored as long as the skins are 'set', meaning
that they do not rub off when harvested: harvest them in July
and August, having cut down the foliage to stop continued
growth. Maincrops are stored for use over winter. Lift them
in dry conditions during September and October, and ensure
they are dry before storing. Put all potatoes to be stored into
a paper sack and store in a cool, dark, frost-free area.

FIRST EARLY VARIETIES INCLUDE Jersey Royal,
Rocket and Duke of York. Harvest as you need them and eat
fresh. When the first flowers appear there should be edible
tubers underneath. First earlies are less likely to encounter
pest problems as they are lifted so much earlier in the year
than the other types.

SECOND EARLIES AND SALAD POTATOES
include Belle de Fontenay, Charlotte and Ratte. Harvest from
July to August as needed and eat fresh. They should be ready

to harvest from the beginning of July onwards – harvest a few to check their size and, if they are too small, leave them for a couple more weeks. These varieties are best dug up as required, as the harvest season for salad potatoes is not long.

MAINCROP VARIETIES INCLUDE Maris Piper, Romano, Cara and King Edward. Harvest from September onwards after the foliage has died back and, on heavy soils, don't leave it too late as slugs will have a field day!

PLANT SEED POTATOES when the soil is warm enough, traditionally around Easter. If the soil is wet, wait a week or two as they will only rot in damp ground. Dig a trench to a spade's depth and add organic matter to the bottom. Some people also add shredded newspaper, which helps to keep the crop 'clean' (free from blemishes), but this isn't essential. Place the seed potatoes in the bottom of the trench, shoot side up, 30 cm apart for earlies and 40 cm for maincrop, before filling in the trench with soil. Leave a bigger distance between the rows for maincrop varieties.

POTATOES LIKE PLENTY OF SUN, so don't plant them in frost-prone sites, as frost can damage the developing leaves. If you're starting up a vegetable plot on very weedy ground or old grassland, potatoes may help swamp out weeds

TOP TIP

Early potatoes must never run short of water.
Give them a good drink every week unless you
have had lots of rain.

with their fast-growing, extensive foliage and, for this reason, are often planted to 'clean the ground'.

CHITTING POTATOES means exposing them to light so that they develop shoots. This is done in order to get them into growth before planting them out and it gets them started earlier once in the ground. Seed potatoes are available from garden centres in January and February, so you can start chitting from late January in warmer parts of the country or in February in cooler areas, about six weeks before you intend to plant them out. Arranged on a seed tray or in egg boxes and placed on a cool window-sill, potatoes will start to sprout fat green buds within a couple of weeks — the exact timing depends on the variety. Before planting the classic advice is to rub out all but one or two shoots to get larger potatoes, but it is not strictly necessary.

POISONOUS PLANTS

Potatoes belong to the Solanaceae family, which includes deadly nightshade, tomatoes, tobacco, petunias, aubergines and peppers. Potatoes naturally produce solanine, a glycoalkaloid which acts as a defence mechanism against insects, diseases and predators. In high concentrations it is poisonous to humans. When potato tubers are exposed to light, they turn green and increase glycoalkaloid production. The green colour is from chlorophyll and is itself harmless. However, it is an indication that an increased level of solanine may be present. Some diseases, such as potato blight, can dramatically increase glycoalkaloid levels. In potato tubers 30–80 per cent of the solanine develops in and close to the skin, so if there are any small green parts in your potatoes cut these off; if the whole potato is green, throw it away.

EARTHING UP encourages underground shoots and therefore more potatoes. It also protects the emerging leaves from frost, helps to guard against blight spores, and lastly, and most importantly, it prevents the potatoes from turning green. The greener the potato, the higher the level of solanine, which in high concentrations is poisonous. Earthing up simply means covering the emerging leaves with soil by drawing it up from between the rows with a hoe or rake and covering all but the tops. It can be done as soon as the plants are about 15 cm tall.

POTATOES IN CONTAINERS. Barrels, large pots and compost bags can be used to plant early and salad potatoes. Make sure that there is adequate drainage in the container and then put in around 15 cm of compost. Add the seed potatoes and cover with another 15 cm of compost. As leaves begin to show through, add more compost and continue this process at intervals until the container will not hold any more. Then allow the plant to grow normally and when the pot is ready to harvest you should find that your container is full of potatoes. For really early crops the container can be grown under cover for a few weeks, then placed outside in May.

A FEW POTATO PROBLEMS

POTATO BLIGHT is cause by a fungus, *Phytophthora infestans*, which needs very high humidity and mild temperatures, day and night, to thrive. The initial signs are the development of small dark areas on the leaves. White threads appear on the underside. The stems may also develop dark brown patches at the points where leaves join them. Infected tubers have brownish discoloration and the flesh has a marbled appearance before rotting away.

COMMON SCAB is caused by a bacterium and is worst in dry conditions: watering well while tubers are developing will decrease the risk of infection. Levels of occurrence are also lower in slightly acid soils. Scab is superficial — it does not affect yield but it is unattractive and makes peeling more of a chore. Some varieties are more susceptible than others and adding plenty of organic matter at planting may help.

SLUGS are a common problem in potatoes. Damage shows up as odd-shaped holes on the surface, leading into large holes in the actual tuber and is more common in potatoes planted in heavy, wet soil. A late harvest may expose your crop to greater risk as slugs are more active in late autumn.

HISTORY OF THE POTATO

The potato or 'papa' originates from the Andes and grows wild there. There is evidence that the cultivation of edible potatoes began over 8000 years ago and today Andean farmers grow over 400 varieties.

No one really knows who brought the potato to England. Accounts of Columbus's first voyage to the Americas in 1492 mention that the Indians served up a cultivated boiled root 'not unlike chestnut in taste'. By the late sixteenth century potatoes were being cultivated in Spain and Italy, and they reached Vienna in about 1588. In the Netherlands in the same year Clusius (of tulip fame, see page 17) mentioned that he had received a couple of tubers but was uncertain whether they had originated in America or Spain; in England Gerard appears to have been growing something similar in 1597, although he claimed his tubers came from Virginia.

TOMATOES

A good tomato should be warm, smell musty and fruity,
and dribble seeds and juice when cut or bitten into.

MONTY DON
The Complete Gardener

There are many varieties of tomatoes, from cherry to large beefsteak, indoor or outdoor, and which ones you choose to grow is a matter of personal taste.

TOMATOES ARE TENDER PLANTS and, if you intend to grow them outside, they need to be started off indoors fairly early in spring. Not too early, though, or they will be big enough to go out before it is warm enough for them.

March is a good time to sow. It's often helpful to cover the pot with some cling film, which prevents water loss and creates a mini-greenhouse effect for the plants to germinate in if you don't have a propagator.

TOP TIP
Putting almost ripe tomatoes in a paper bag with a banana will speed up the ripening process.

TOMATOES NEED 'PRICKING OUT' as soon as a pair of true leaves appears. They grow so quickly that this generally happens within two weeks of planting. Fill individual 9 cm pots with fresh compost, tap each pot to settle the compost, water it and then leave to drain. Insert the pointed end of a pencil or a finger alongside a seedling and then, holding the seed leaves (these will have smooth edges and look different from the true leaves) between thumb and forefinger, gently push under the seedling and, at the same time, lift it out. Make a hole in the compost in a new pot, insert the seedling and gently firm it in. Keep these pots uncovered, well watered and on the window-sill for at least another month.

HARDENING OFF AND PLANTING OUT. Tomatoes can be planted out at the end of May or, in colder areas, the beginning of June. But first they need to be acclimatized to the weather outside. On warm sunny days, from about ten days before you intend to plant them out, take the pots outside for the day and bring them in at night (to avoid any risk of late frosts). Do this for about a week and then, a few days before planting out, leave them out overnight as well.

TOMATOES NEED A SUNNY SPOT and can be grown in a container against a sunny wall or in the open ground, but they need good, well-manured soil, water and plenty of food at the right time. Plant them deep, right up to the first set of leaves. This will force the stem to sprout extra roots, which will increase the plant's chances of getting more water and nutrients from the soil. Water them daily. A liquid tomato feed once a week after the fruits have formed nourishes the plants just when they need it most to produce fruit. This is especially important if they are grown in containers, but not so critical when they are grown in the open ground.

UNLESS YOU ARE GROWING A BUSH TOMATO, the aim is to create a single-stemmed plant. To do this, snap out shoots that grow in leaf joints and when your plant has produced four sets of flowering trusses, pinch out the growing tip. This will ensure all its energy goes into producing fruit.

TOMATO FLOWERS SELF-POLLINATE FREELY. However, indoor plants benefit from being gently shaken to dislodge the pollen. Misting flowers can also help fruit set.

TOMATO HISTORY

Tomatoes originate from South America and were originally cultivated by the Aztecs and Incas as early as 700 AD. It is assumed that the Spaniards brought them to Europe from Mexico. They arrived in Britain during the late 1500s, when one writer described how 'tomates' were 'good to eate', full of juice and gave good flavour to sauces.

In Europe the plant became associated with more poisonous members of the Solanaceae family, to which it belongs. These include henbane, mandrake and deadly nightshade. The French botanist Tournefort gave the tomato the botanical name *Lycopersicon esculentum*. Lycopersicon translates as 'wolf peach' — 'peach' because it was round and luscious and 'wolf' because it was considered poisonous. Up until the end of the eighteenth century, physicians warned against eating tomatoes, fearing they caused not only appendicitis but also stomach cancer from tomato skins adhering to the lining of the stomach.

During the French Revolution the citizens of Paris wore red caps as a mark of faith in the Republic. A zealous chef suggested that the faithful should eat red food to demonstrate their devotion to the revolution. At the time the tomato was known to be popular in various southern parts of Europe but was not recommended by the French aristocracy, making it the perfect mascot for the revolutionaries. It quickly became popular and was served as a stewed side dish and in summer salads.

The story goes that in 1820 a Colonel Johnson of Massachusetts once and for all proved tomatoes safe for consumption. He stood on the steps of the Salem courthouse and consumed an entire basket of the fruit without suffering any ill effects; in the process attracting a crowd of over 2000 people who were certain he was committing public suicide. In fact, tomatoes contain lycopene, which is acknowledged as being an agent in releasing free radicals that help fight and prevent cancers.

TOP TIP

*If you have lots of green tomatoes at the end
of summer and you don't want to ripen them
indoors, use them to make chutney.*

BUSH TOMATOES. On seed packets tomatoes are often
described as bush or 'determinate', which means that when
they reach a certain size they stop growing and do not need
to have any side shoots removed nor to be staked. In practice
it is a good idea to give them some support, as they do tend
to sprawl and may fall over with the weight of fruit. Their
period of harvest is shorter than that of the cordon types.

CORDON TOMATOES or 'indeterminate' tomatoes
will keep on growing until they die. They need supporting
from the time of planting out and their side shoots should
be pinched out regularly. They take up less space than bush
tomatoes and are therefore good for a small greenhouse.
Their growth needs to be stopped by pinching out the top in
early September so that the energy of the plant is not wasted
forming new fruit. The fruit ripens over a long period.

RIPENING TOMATOES. Being left with too many green
tomatoes at the end of summer can be a bit of a problem, so to
speed ripening remove leaves which are shading the tomatoes
so that light and air can get to the fruit. Autumn frosts will kill
any plants outside, so harvest them before this has a chance to
happen and bring them indoors. Whole trusses of tomatoes,
both red and green, can be hung up in a warm dry spot and
will continue to ripen.

FRUIT

Nothing tastes better than sun-ripened fruit
freshly picked from your own plants.

JONATHAN KEYTE
Gardening With the Experts

TREE FRUIT

All fruit trees are grown on rootstocks. This means that a plant
is grafted or joined onto another plant — the rootstock — from
the same family. It is the rootstock that determines how big the
tree will grow.

GRAFTING IS AN ANCIENT ART. It's been around
for 10,000 years and hasn't changed much. Quite simply,
if you plant the seed of an apple or any other fruit, you won't
know what the resulting fruit will be. If you want more of the
same then you have to take a bit of bud from the tree, known
as the scion, and put it onto the root of something else. In this
way you can ensure that you get the fruit that you want, while
also influencing the size of the resulting tree, because the
growing vigour comes from the rootstock you use.

Grafting enables any fruit to be introduced from anywhere.
You can even graft different varieties onto the same rootstock —
the result will be one tree that bears different fruit.

HOW DO YOU GRAFT? Amateur gardeners don't usually
do their own grafting — it's a professional's job — but what
happens is that the bud wood of one tree is cut from the
stem, inserted into a slit made on the stem of another and
then sealed with a plastic tie or, traditionally, with wax.

In Tudor times wax was a precious commodity, so they sealed the graft with 'pug', a disgusting mixture of dung and soil — the same mixture that was used to build houses. It produced a kind of mortar that sealed the graft and prevented the water from getting in and spoiling it. The word grafting comes from the Greek *grapheion*, a writing implement, and that's the size of the wood you need for grafting — pencil-sized.

PLANT FRUIT TREES IN SUN and in a sheltered position. They do not like windy sites or to go short of water, especially when the fruits are forming.

APPLES

Apple trees are sold on rootstocks which have 'M' numbers categorizing dwarf, semi-dwarf and vigorous trees.

Dwarf trees have the numbers M27 (1.5–1.8m) and M9 (2.4–3m).

Semi-dwarf have the numbers M26 (2.4–3.6m) and MM106 (3.6–5.4m).

Vigorous have the numbers MM111 (6–9m) and M25 (over 9m).

The dwarfing rootstocks are suitable for growing in pots; semi-dwarf apples won't take up too much space and are suitable for small gardens; vigorous rootstocks are suitable for open ground and orchards, and will take a few years to produce fruit.

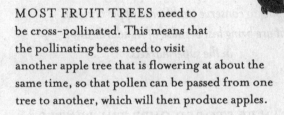

FROST MEANS NO FRUIT and for apple-growing this simply means choosing a variety that comes into flower late on in spring, when all risk of frost has passed.

MOST FRUIT TREES need to be cross-pollinated. This means that the pollinating bees need to visit another apple tree that is flowering at about the same time, so that pollen can be passed from one tree to another, which will then produce apples.

APPLES AS APHRODISIAC

Apples have traditionally been invested with powerful aphrodisiac qualities and this is probably why they were eaten at the end of a meal, as a precursor to more pleasures to come. Along with pears, pomegranates, figs, prunes, almonds and oranges, in Greek, Roman and Persian culture apples were closely associated with the art of love. On her wedding night a Persian girl would be allowed to eat nothing but apples and camel's marrow. The apple was sacred to the Greek goddess of love, Aphrodite, and her Roman counterpart Venus. In ancient Greece the unattached would hurl apples at each other as a sign of romantic interest. In Roman times banquets were served in outdoor dining rooms amidst living apple and other fruit trees in tubs, which could be wheeled around.

The Tudor and Stuart courts took on this idea and defied the English weather by adjourning to separate banqueting houses in the garden where they could eat fresh fruit and other sweet foods. Banqueting houses allowed guests to sustain themselves without the inhibiting attentions of servants and the 'second table' of fruit was invented to 'prolong the party'.

TOP TIP

Research local varieties when choosing an apple tree. The fruit will almost certainly be tastier than anything you can buy in the shops and you will be helping to conserve traditional apple varieties that are being lost because of standardization in the supermarkets.

APPLES CAN BE STORED OVER THE WINTER and will last well as long as the fruit is blemish-free. One bad, all bad is the mantra for storing fruit. Apples need plenty of air, a constant temperature of 3–7°C and darkness, so a shed or garage is ideal. Crates are perfect for storing as they allow air to circulate and they can be stacked, but you can also wrap apples in newspaper or put them in polythene bags as long as you pierce the bags to prevent condensation.

THE MOTHER OF ALL ORCHARDS

Henry VIII had a huge influence on the fruit we grow today. He loved fruit and filled his royal gardens with it. But the Tudors were suspicious of raw fruit and mostly ate it boiled or roasted. Henry employed a Master of Fruiterers, a certain Richard Harris, and sent him abroad to bring back the newest and best varieties of apples, pears and cherries then growing in Europe. In 1533 Harris brought over numerous grafts and started a model orchard at Teynham in Kent. So Henry's love of fruit was the beginning of what we now call the Garden of England.

PEARS

Pears, like apples, are grafted onto rootstocks. They are naturally very deep-rooting and so are often grafted onto quince trees, which are more shallow-rooted.

They are also very similar to apples in their cultivation requirements, but need a bit more mollycoddling. They flower early, so can get frosted, and need more warmth and sunlight than apples, so it is best to plant them in a very sheltered spot.

THE PERFECT SOLUTION for a small garden is to grow pears against a wall or trellis. Not only are they protected, but they will also take up less space. However, like apples, pears need to be cross-pollinated, so growing two varieties is often the answer if there is no pear tree in a neighbouring garden.

PEARS ARE A DELICIOUS FRUIT and should be harvested by gently cupping the fruit and lifting. A pear that is ready for harvesting will simply fall into your hands. At this stage they are not quite ready for eating. Pears ripen from the inside out, so need to be stored upright for a couple of weeks after picking. Once the top of the fruit feels soft when gently pressed, they are ready to eat.

TOP TIP
Pear trees blossom early, so plant them against a warm wall or in a sheltered spot to prevent the flowers from being damaged in the spring.

BERRIES

All sorts of berries have become extremely popular because of their huge health benefits. They are also some of the easiest fruits to grow in the UK, requiring very little attention and producing masses of fruit each year.

Berries can be classified into two categories: cane fruit and bush fruit. Raspberries are cane fruit; bush fruit includes blackcurrants, redcurrants and gooseberries.

Currants — red, white and black

All need similar growing conditions and all three can be grown happily together. Look for two-year-old plants which have at least two stems of pencil thickness.

Blackcurrants are extremely rich in Vitamin C and are said to help the prevention of joint inflammation, eyestrain and urinary infections. One bush has the potential to produce about 5 kg of fruit per year. Plant in late autumn or early spring in a sunny part of the garden in soil that is moist but not waterlogged, with lots of manure or compost dug in. Plant blackcurrants 2.5 cm deeper than they were grown in their containers, as this will encourage new shoots from the base of the plants.

Dig a large hole to allow the roots to spread easily and mix some garden compost or manure into the bottom of the hole. Take the bush out of its pot and tease out the roots a little from the compost or, if it is a bare-root plant, spread the roots evenly around the base of the hole, making sure the bush is upright. Return the soil, firm around the bush and keep well watered. Once planted, cut back the existing shoots to one bud from the base.

Prune the bush in winter a year or two after planting, once it has seven or eight good branches. Remove a third of the branches down to ground level or to a strong new side stem.

Red and white currants should be trained as an open-centred, goblet-shaped bush which allows light and air to flow freely around the branches and makes picking easier. Prune back by half after planting and thereafter prune in winter, from November to February. First remove any dead, diseased or damaged stems and any overcrowded stems in the middle of the bush. Then shorten the main stems to about half their size and shorten the side shoots to about 5 cm or just above a bud.

All currants start to ripen from mid-summer and this is when they are vulnerable to bird attack, so throw a net over each bush to keep the fruit for yourself. If you don't net them you don't get them is the watchword for most fruit crops.

GOOSEBERRIES got their name as they were used to make a sharp-tasting sauce to accompany roast goose. The first fruit of the year to ripen, they can be ready to pick as early as mid May and the plants, although thorny, live for a long time and are very tough.

Plant them as two- or three-year-old bushes, cut back all the main branches by half and then prune again the first winter after planting, removing any branches that are within 20 cm of the ground and any that cross over in the middle. You should end up with a goblet shape of six to eight main branches. Cut side shoots back to two buds.

Fruit can be thinned once it is semi-ripe in May by removing every other berry and leaving the remainder to grow bigger and ripen for picking fresh in July. Gooseberries taste sharper when they are young and get sweeter as they ripen. Early pickings can be used for cooking.

RASPBERRIES are incredibly easy to grow and, if pruned once a year, will produce masses of fruit. They prefer a sunny spot in well-drained, sandy soils. Prepare the soil by digging in plenty of organic matter such as garden compost, and removing the roots of any perennial weeds.

Most raspberry plants are sold as bundles of one-year-old canes in late autumn and winter. If you have enough space, consider growing both summer and autumn varieties to prolong the fruiting season.

Put in a sturdy framework of posts and wires before planting the canes in the ground. Space the canes 50–100 cm apart, cut them down to ground level and water well. Tie them in as soon as the canes are long enough to need support on the framework. For beginners to raspberry growing, 'Autumn Bliss' is a good variety to start with, as it is easy to look after and extremely tasty.

STRAWBERRIES
(NOT REALLY BERRIES)

A strawberry pot is the ultimate solution for gardeners who think their patch is too small for fruit. All right, you won't become self-sufficient, but the pleasure of picking a fresh strawberry or two for your morning cornflakes is well worth the space taken up by a single flowerpot.

ALAN TITCHMARSH
How to be a Gardener: Secrets of Success

Strawberries belong to the rose family and are the only fruits that have seeds on the outside rather than inside. They are another extremely healthy fruit, being rich in vitamin C, a good source of folic acid and high in fibre. It is possible to plant a number of varieties so that you have fruit from early summer to autumn. There are early, mid and late strawberries, as well as perpetual varieties which crop continuously. Good nurseries will offer advice on the best ones to grow.

Plant strawberries in a sunny or partly shaded part of the garden in well-drained soil. Planting in the autumn gives them time to establish in the soil, overwinter and then grow strongly in the spring, giving a crop of fruit that summer. If you plant in the spring you will need to remove the flowers so that the plant's energy can be concentrated towards developing roots and a sturdy structure which will produce fruit the following year.

Place strawberry plants about 40 cm apart in rows, leaving 30 cm between the rows and then, in late spring, just as the flowers finish and the fruits begin to form, mulch the surrounding soil with straw to protect the fruit from mud splashes. Net the fruit to prevent birds eating it and check regularly for slugs.

STRAWBERRY LORE

Wild or woodland strawberries, *Fragaria vesca,* have occurred
naturally in the British Isles since the Ice Age and for centuries
they were the only strawberries available. The fruit is normally
small but has a delicious flavour.

Strawberries were cultivated by the Romans as early as 200 BC
and in medieval times they were regarded as an aphrodisiac:
a soup made of strawberries, borage and soured cream was
traditionally served to newlyweds at their wedding breakfast.
Cultivated strawberries were known in England by Tudor times:
there are records of plants being supplied to the gardens of
Hampton Court during the reign of Henry VIII.

In the sixteenth century, strawberries were sold in cone-
shaped straw baskets, making them one of the earliest packaged
foods, and in the late nineteenth century they were being grown
on the outskirts of London and transported into Covent Garden
by women who had begun harvesting at daybreak. The fruit was
put into baskets weighing over 14 kg and then placed on top of
a cushion on the women's heads for 'jogging' into market.

The ancient Roman practice of using strawberries as a natural
tooth whitener is still being championed today. Crush a ripe
strawberry with a little baking powder, brush onto the teeth and
leave for five minutes before brushing again and rinsing.

After the harvest cut the foliage down to about 10 cm to stimulate the growth of new leaves, and remove any old straw or mulch to reduce the risk of disease.

NEW STRAWBERRIES FOR NOTHING. The straw-berry's habit of producing runners, which are new plants at the end of long stems, can be exploited by pegging these plantlets down onto a pot of compost, where they will take root. Once roots have formed, the long stem can be cut from the mother plant and planted out in the open soil – the cycle of growth then begins again. Strawberry plants need to be renewed every three years, and these new plants are invaluable for the creation and continuation of the strawberry supply. Don't plant strawberries where they have been growing within the last four years, as this may make them prone to soil-borne diseases.

FIGS

Figs are hardy deciduous shrubs which in the wild can grow to 9 metres, although cultivated varieties tend to be smaller. They have a tendency to spread outwards rather than up and so will usually form a bush rather than a tall tree, which makes them ideal plants for urban gardens.

TREAT THEM MEAN. Figs will fruit much better if you restrict the root growth. This means they are ideal for growing in containers. They can even be planted within a leather bag or pot and then buried to restrict the root growth. Alternatively, dig a square hole by a south-facing wall, line the hole with paving slabs placed on their edges, and plant the fig in its concrete-lined pit. Planted directly into the ground figs make lots of leaf growth and become large without producing much fruit.

The fruits form during the summer as tiny green figlets, normally near the bases of the leaf stalks. These persist over the winter after the leaves drop and then ripen the following summer. Only in hot climates can you expect figs to form and ripen the same year. However, when the leaves drop you must go over the plant and pull off any figlets that are larger than pea-sized. Although it is tempting to leave them, they will not survive the winter and when the plant comes to life the following spring they will steal nourishment from the smaller figlets before rotting and dropping off the tree.

AS THE FIGLETS GROW, tiny flowers form inside the fruit which are completely hidden from the outside. In hot climates the flowers are pollinated by a tiny fig wasp which lives inside the developing fruit. After a time the fig will ripen and soften and, depending on the variety, can have a skin that is anything from green or yellow through to purple. All parts of the fruit are edible, including the skin, and in pollinated varieties the fruit will be full of tiny crunchy seeds, which make them taste slightly nutty.

DON'T PICK FIGS before they are ripe — they will not ripen off the tree and you will end up disappointed. 'Brown Turkey' is the best variety for the British climate. Varieties for cold climates are self-fertile — they do not need a fig wasp to pollinate the fruit.

NEW PLANTS CAN BE RAISED from cuttings taken from established trees. Take them in summer from the new, soft wood formed that year; they should be about 15 cm long with several leaf buds. Plant in ordinary potting compost and keep in a moist, shady position until they have rooted, which will take about 2–3 months.

A FIGGY FACT: Figs have more fibre than any other fruit and when dried contain up to 50 per cent sugar.

HERBS

Herbs have been used in medicine since the earliest recorded times: the Chinese knew their virtues over 4000 years ago and fragments of herbal remedies from Egypt have been found dating from about the same period. Papyri exist for areas of medicine such as gynaecology, surgery and diseases of the eye. The treatments they recommend involve herbs and minerals that scientists today regard as being effective. The Egyptians realized, for instance, that aloe vera relieved headaches and soothed burns; basil was good for the heart; garlic and mint eased flatulence and aided digestion; parsley was a diuretic and thyme was a pain reliever — all of which have since been proved to be true.

MANY PLANTS with aromatic leaves, which includes many herbs, grow in hot environments. On warm days the leaves release an oily vapour which lowers their temperature and provides protection against the scorching effect of the sun. In the early part of the twentieth century, experiments were carried out into this cooling effect. Various shrubs were planted against sun-baked brick walls and the temperature of the wall monitored. It was discovered that rosemary was able to keep the wall cooler than any other shrub; thyme had the second strongest cooling effect, and third came lavender.

OILS FOUND IN SCENTED LEAVES are repulsive or even toxic to pests, so they help to defend the plant against attack. Chemical companies are interested in making use of these natural insecticides: for example, it's been discovered that many insects don't like the oil in thyme leaves, so there are now flea collars for cats and dogs on the market made with thyme oil. Some plants have developed defence mechanisms that not only repel pests, but simultaneously attract other insects that prey on the pests.

PLANTS COMMUNICATE WITH EACH OTHER by giving off aromatic vapours: if one plant has been attacked by pests, others around it can detect the chemicals given off by the victim, and they respond by producing protective chemicals themselves.

SOME AROMATIC PLANTS store their oil deep within the leaves, so that you have to crush them quite hard to release the perfume: an example is the bay leaf. Others, like rosemary, store the oil nearer the surface so that you can smell it by pressing or rubbing the leaf. Yet others, like thyme, store their oil on the surface, so that the scent is released just by warmth.

LEAF SCENTS ARE MORE PERSISTENT than flower scents. Most flower scents fade when the petals die, but the scents of leaves often become more intense as the leaves dry.

GARDENING IN LITERATURE

The earliest known medical textbook is the five-volume *De Materia Medica*, written in the first century AD by the Greek physician Dioscorides, who featured the medical uses of herbs. These writings were introduced to Europe by the Romans and later by Moorish herbalists. Hundred of years later, the English produced their own 'herballs', most notably those by the Reverend Dr William Turner and John Gerard in the sixteenth century and Nicholas Culpeper in the seventeenth.

The first English gardening book is said to have been written by Jon Gardener (or Gardyner). *The Feate of Gardening* survives as five manuscript pages written in verse. It can be dated to 1440 but it has been argued that it was written about a hundred years earlier by Edward III's gardener, Jon Penalowne, during the 1350s. Whoever the author was, there are two surviving manuscripts describing one hundred herbs, a quarter of which are native to Britain, with sections on trees, grafting, viticulture, onions, parsley and coleworts (greens).

In 1557 Thomas Tusser's *Five Hundred Points of Good Husbandry* offered lists of what to sow and harvest month by month in easy-to-read verse. 'Wife, into thy garden', he orders in spring.

> For garden best
> Is south southwest
> Good tilth brings seedes
> Evil tilture, weedes.

Thomas Hill was the great gardening innovator of the sixteenth century. In his book *The Gardeners' Labyrinth* (1577), he addressed wives (who took charge of the kitchen garden) on the correct way to plan a garden. Facing southeast and sloping slightly to catch the full morning sun, it should be divided into quarters, each containing a number of raised beds, four to five feet wide. In the centre should be a 'dipping pool' for watering.

GROWING HERBS

Herbs are wild plants and so the most successful way to grow them is to give them conditions that are as close as possible to those of their original environment. As a general rule, that means a dry and sunny place: think of a baked hillside in Provence and you won't go far wrong.

GRIT, GRIT AND MORE GRIT is the maxim for growing herbs on heavy soils. Most will thrive if a handful of grit is added to the planting hole and none likes soil that is waterlogged or permanently wet.

HERB INVADERS. Mint and lemon balm are wonderful herbs to grow for cooking and tea infusions, but they can take over the whole garden and inhibit other herbs. Grow them in a pot which can either be positioned wherever you like or sunk into the soil. This will restrict their root growth and prevent them from spreading where they are not wanted.

GOING TO SEED. Annual herbs like coriander and dill can quickly go to seed in hot weather, which means that they concentrate their energy on making flowers and seeds rather than leaves. Drought conditions can also cause this. These herbs may appreciate a bit of shading and regular harvesting to prevent this happening.

TOP TIP
Plant herbs just outside the kitchen door.
They'll be convenient for picking, and the scent
will waft past you every time you go outside.

ESSENTIAL HERBS
FOR THE KITCHEN

The choice of what to grow is enormous and it has to be a personal one — there is no point in having herbs that you are not going to use. However, a basic starter kit might include the following.

BASIL originated in India, where it is considered sacred. It now grows wild in the Mediterranean and is a key ingredient in the cuisine of that area, particularly in pizza, pasta, pesto and as an addition to salads — the perfect partner for tomatoes. In the UK it needs quite a bit of warmth and shelter from cold wind.

There are many varieties, each
with slightly different flavours:

Sweet basil is the most popular variety in the UK.
It grows to a height of 75 cm.

Cinnamon basil comes from Mexico. It has a slight flavour
of cinnamon and grows to a height of 45 cm.

Lemon basil has a mild lemon flavour and is a great
accompaniment to fish. It grows to 30 cm.

Purple basil is similar to sweet basil, except for its
luscious, dark purple leaves. It can reach 75 cm.

CHIVES are a versatile herb with a mild onion flavour (they are a member of the Allium family, which also includes onions and garlic). They can be chopped up and added to salads and a variety of potato dishes, including mashed and baked potatoes, or used as an accompaniment to fish and eggs. They are tastiest when used fresh, but can be frozen for use throughout winter.

Chives grow well in pots and make a good decorative edging to a herb garden. They need regular harvesting: the best way to do this is with scissors, cutting the spears down to within a few centimetres of the ground, which allows them to grow back.

TOP TIP
For winter supplies, dig up a few roots of chives or mint and pot up in autumn for growing on the kitchen windowsill.

CORIANDER is popular in Asian cooking. Both the seeds and the leaves of the plant can be used, and offer two distinct flavours. The seeds are slightly lemony; they are often ground and used as a spice. The leaves (also known as cilantro) have a slightly bitter taste and can be cooked in Asian dishes and breads, or used raw as a garnish.

Coriander enjoys a sunny position but appreciates a little shade during the hottest part of the day. Sow varieties that have been specifically bred for either seed or leaf: 'Cilantro' is an excellent choice for leaf production.

Coriander is best grown from seed sown directly into the soil in spring or autumn, as it is quick to run to seed in hot weather. Rake the soil so it's level and sow seeds 4 cm apart in drills 1 cm deep. Germination takes up to three weeks; once young plants are visible thin them to 20 cm apart to allow them to grow to their full size. Water them in dry periods and ensure the soil never dries out. If flowers develop, remove them immediately – this ensures the plants focus their energy on growing new leaves. Re-sow coriander every three weeks to ensure a continual supply during the summer.

Harvest the leaves by cutting each one off the stem or snip whole stems if necessary. Both the leaves and the stalks can be used. The flowers need to be dry before you harvest the seed. Cut the stems, place the heads of coriander upside down in a paper bag and hang the bag up for three weeks in a cool, dry place. Shake the bag and the seeds will fall to the bottom.

MINT is a hardy perennial and a voracious grower. It will do well in both sunny and shady parts of the garden and is worth growing for the flavour it brings to new potatoes and infused in hot water for mint tea. There are so many decorative and subtly different flavours to be had from mint – peppermint, spearmint, pineapple mint and many more – that it is purely down to personal taste which variety you grow.

Mint is tolerant of most conditions, but it prefers a well-drained, fertile soil with a fair amount of moisture. Remove any flowers that appear, to keep the plant producing leaves right up until autumn. Leaves can be cut as required but always from the top, which will encourage new leaves to sprout from the sides.

Mint can also be propagated from its roots. Simply take a piece of root and pot it up in a small container, keeping it well watered. This is a great way of ensuring a supply of fresh mint over the winter, as the container can be brought indoors and kept on a kitchen window-sill.

OREGANO originates in the Mediterranean and is closely related to marjoram: it is, in fact, wild marjoram but has a more intense flavour. Both like a well-drained site in full sun and will thrive on a sandy or chalky soil. They are tolerant of most conditions, requiring very little care other than regular watering of new plants until they get established.

Harvest the leaves in July, just before the flowers appear: if you wait until after that, the leaves can taste bitter. However, removing the flower heads before they open will encourage the plant to produce more leaves and not flowers, which means that the leaves will retain their flavour and ensure a harvest right up until November. For dried leaves, pick on a dry day and store in a dark, dry, warm place until they are crumbly in texture. Then remove to an airtight container, where they will retain their flavour for up to six months.

PARSLEY needs a fairly rich soil in order to thrive. Once established, however, it is a low-maintenance plant that requires very little attention. It is a biennial, which means it will flower and produce seeds in its second year of growth, so an annual sowing is needed to maintain a constant supply.

There are two main types: flat-leaf (Italian) parsley resembles coriander and has a milder taste than curled parsley, which is often used as a garnish. Both varieties are very hardy and will survive the winter outside.

Grown from seed, parsley can take a few weeks to germinate because it needs quite high temperatures. It is often easier to grow parsley from plants bought in the garden centre, or to sow seeds indoors in March and keep in a warm room until

TOP TIP
To speed up germination, soak parsley seed in warm water overnight before sowing.

the plants are ready to be
hardened off (see page 101)
and transplanted outside.
Unlike many herbs, parsley
will grow quite well in shade.

Harvest the leaves with
scissors, taking care not to remove
all of them, as this will hamper
the plant's growth.

ROSEMARY is a decorative
herb originating from the
Mediterranean and bears small
blue or white flowers from early to
late spring. It is a hardy evergreen
perennial shrub that thrives in
good soil in full sun and can live
for up to 20 years, requiring little attention. Some varieties
have been bred to sprawl, others, like 'Miss Jessop's Upright',
to grow upright, when they can reach a height of 2 metres.
Rosemary will tolerate most growing conditions, as long as it
is not waterlogged. Prune every autumn, then dry the prunings
and keep them in a sealed container.

Sometimes rosemary dies back in the early spring and it is
best to cut out the dying stems promptly as the rest of the plant
may follow suit.

SAGE is used in traditional British cuisine to make stuffing
and to flavour meat dishes, but it is native to the Mediterranean.
It grows like a shrub and keeps most of its leaves over winter,
enjoying a sunny position and a well-drained soil. It is a
wonderful herb to grow in borders, its blue flowers and suede-
like leaves mingling well with other plants.

There are plenty of varieties to try, including purple- and variegated-leaved ones, with a range of differently coloured flowers. After the flowers die down prune sage back to half its size, using secateurs. Sage loses some of its flavour after about three years, but cuttings can be taken to make new, fresh plants.

Sage is best used fresh, although the leaves can be placed in a plastic bag and frozen for use throughout the winter. They can also be dried by harvesting them on a dry day and storing in a warm, dry room until they are crumbly to the touch. Transfer the crumbled leaves to an airtight container out of direct sunlight.

THYME, originally from southern Europe, is an unassuming little plant with attractive foliage and flowers and an abundance of varieties to choose from. It is easy to care for, very hardy and tolerates all sorts of abuse. It doesn't even mind being trodden on, which is why it is rather lovely to grow a thyme carpet near a path so that the aroma is released on footfall. It is also beloved by bees.

TOP TIP

Thyme can be used for ground cover and is happy to grow in the cracks between paving stones or rocks.

After three years, thyme will become woody and produce fewer leaves. At this stage it should be dug up and divided to make new plants.

Thyme may be harvested throughout the year. However, its leaves taste best in June and July. Simply remove the sprigs using scissors or secateurs.

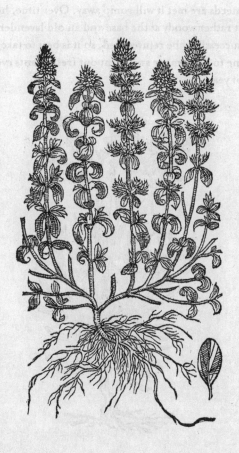

LAVENDER – THE MAINSTAY
OF THE HERB GARDEN

Lavender is not often used in the kitchen, but is an essential element of the herb garden as an ornamental and because of its many other uses – for cut flowers, lavender bags and the sheer indulgence of crushing a leaf and breathing in its aroma. Lavender, like most herbs, loves gritty soil and full sun and if those needs are met it will romp away. Over time, however, it can get rather woody at the base and an old lavender plant cannot successfully be rejuvenated, so it is best to take cuttings from June to September and plant out fresh plants every couple of years.

LAVENDER CUTTINGS Select several young shoots with no flowers and pull each shoot sharply downwards so that it comes away from the plant with a slight 'heel' at the bottom. Take off some of the lower leaves, leaving a bare stem, and push the cuttings around the edge of a pot of very sandy compost. Water them in and cover the pot with a polythene bag to keep the humidity high. After a couple of weeks check the bottom of the pot to see if any roots are visible and, if they are, remove the polythene bag and then wait a few more weeks before separating the cuttings. Pot them up individually.

COMFREY – THE WONDER FERTILIZER

Comfrey is not often used as a culinary herb either, but it has long been known in Britain for its medicinal properties. Once known as knitbone, it was traditionally thought to assist in healing broken bones and clearing up skin complaints, and many people still use comfrey-based products for those purposes.

But its use as a fertilizer is the main reason to grow it in the vegetable garden. Comfrey contains high levels of the basic nutrients that plants need – nitrogen (for leaf growth), phosphorus (for roots and germination) and potassium (for flowers and fruit) – all of which it draws up from the deep via its extensive root system. As such it can be useful as an organic food for plants.

Experiments into comfrey's use as a fertilizer were begun in the nineteenth century by a Quaker smallholder, Henry Doubleday, and carried on in the 1950s by Lawrence D Hills, who founded what became Europe's largest organic gardening association, The Henry Doubleday Research Association, now known as Garden Organic. In a measured experiment, Hills found that comfrey had comparable, if not better, amounts of nitrogen, phosphorus and potash compared with commercial liquid feeds made up to the manufacturer's specifications.

TOP TIP
The leaves of comfrey have little hairs on them which can be irritating to the skin, so wear gloves.

In the garden comfrey can be used:

As a compost activator — it not only enriches your heaps but encourages them to heat up.

In the furrow before you plant potatoes: use the first cut of the year, harvested in the spring. A liquid feed can also be good for potatoes, as can chopped, wilted leaves applied as a mulch, before the potato foliage gets too dense for you to be able to spread a mulch effectively.

As a mulch and as a liquid feed for tomatoes, runner and dwarf beans. Fill a barrel or tub with water, add a good handful of comfrey leaves and leave for three to five weeks. It will smell disgusting when finished, but it is very effective.

Mixed with leaf mould to make a base for potting compost.

COMFREY WILL THRIVE IN FULL SUN or in partial to near full shade — there is usually a disused corner that will make a great site for a comfrey bed. Because its roots go down a fair way, it likes deeply dug soils; with light sandy soils, add plenty of organic matter. Being a fleshy plant comfrey needs a lot of water and a soggy patch will be a plus. Plant in March, April, May or September around 60–90 cm apart and the plants will grow quite quickly. When the flowers appear, cut the plants down to about 15 cm from the ground. If you harvest the leaves in spring you can expect three or four more cuts in the course of the year.

CHAPTER THREE

DESIGN

*Having collected, as far as possible, all the information regarding
your particular plot of ground, you can retire to your study with
a pencil and paper, and proceed to plan your new garden.
Here, of course, your own personal taste and artistic ability will
show themselves. No two gardens can ever be exactly similar,
and it would be undesirable if they could.*

M JAMES
The Complete Guide to Home Gardens

STRUCTURING A GARDEN

*It is the spaces between plants and objects that make a garden
interesting, not just the plants themselves. This can be quite a hard
concept to grasp for the organised western mind but in truth it is
simplicity itself. In practice it means getting the proportions right with
the space available, using paths, walls, hedges, trees and every kind of
plant that one wishes to grow so that they make beautiful spaces.*

MONTY DON
The Complete Gardener

Less is more is the first, and probably most important, rule
of garden design. It was the dictum of the German architect
Mies van der Rohe and in garden design terms it means keep
it simple, however small or large the garden may be. The
grandest of gardens have the simplest layout of paths, flower
beds and hard surfaces. A strong structure allows the plants
to tell the story and means that, even in winter, the garden
is good to look at.

The structure of a garden is the framework that divides
up the space. It is often called 'the bones' and can be animate
or inanimate. Inanimate objects such as paths, patios, pergolas,
fences, trellis or obelisks all contribute to structure, whereas
animate structure is provided by the living elements that also
define the garden — hedges, trees and evergreen shrubs.

FOR A GOOD BALANCED DESIGN most designers
would recommend that a third of the garden should be
planting and the other two thirds grass or hard surfaces. This
general principle is based on the classical idea of the 'Golden
Mean' and prevents a space from becoming visually top heavy.

IF YOU ARE DESIGNING A GARDEN FROM scratch
or embarking on a redesign of an existing one, you need to
begin by assessing the space. Ask yourself three things:

[1]

What is the garden to be used for?
Answers might include relaxation, parties,
children's play, growing flowers, vegetables
or both – or any combination
of these.

[2]

What is the aspect of the garden?
Is it shady or open and sunny, overlooked or secluded?
Where does the sun come from?

[3]

How do you want the garden to look?
Formal, restrained, modern, colourful or just
billowing with plants?

The answers to these questions will help you to work out your
priorities and also the conditions you have to work with.

NEXT, FIND OUT WHAT YOU LIKE. Make a mood
board by cutting out or copying pictures that appeal to you
from books and magazines. Stick them onto a large piece of
card and add to the board gradually. Choose plants, gardens,
furniture, patios, containers and even sheds and eventually a
mood and a preference for certain colours and materials will
begin to emerge. Never rush into a garden design. If you are
patient and methodical, you have a better chance of ending
up with something that pleases you.

TOP TIP

*When planning your garden, remember
all your senses — think about scent, colour
and touch in your planting, sow edible
crops and create a feature for the sound
of running water.*

MEASURE OUT THE GARDEN using the back of
the house as a 'base line' (or the front if it is a front garden).
Take various measurements from the house to the end of the
garden; measure the width at intervals from the back of the
house to the end; measure from the corner of the house
diagonally across to the far corner of the garden. Using large-
squared graph paper with each square representing 1 or 2
metres, plot the space on the paper. Mark the position of
windows and doors, then gradually add in all the elements
you want: sitting area, shed, borders, paths and even where
the washing line is to go.

NARROW GARDENS ARE OFTEN THE easiest to
design. A long thin garden can be broken up into different
spaces, divided by hedges or trellis, each with a different
purpose or feel. This gives you the opportunity to have a
formal area as well as an informal one, and to screen off
practical spaces such as the garden shed or the place where you
keep the rubbish bins. A curved and sinuous path with broad
planting spaces on either side running the length of a small
narrow garden makes it feel longer, and if the path leads to
a decorative shed, seating area or focal point, it creates an
interesting 'journey' through the garden.

GARDENS THAT ARE WIDER than they are long are often the most challenging to design, as the whole garden can be seen at once and it is difficult to create any mystery or journey. Adding pergolas over paths and arbours at the end of paths can help — they divide the garden visually without the use of solid hedges or panels. Or, as with a narrow garden, you can create private areas by using trellis. Placing panels along the edge of a patio and covering them with climbers immediately creates a sense of privacy.

> ## TOP TIP
> *Consider doors and windows when designing your garden. A door needs to lead out onto a hard surface like a path or terrace. Key plants and focal points can be lined up to give the best views from windows.*

A FOCAL POINT is something that leads the eye around the garden and acts like an exclamation mark within it. It can be anything, from a large urn placed in a key position, to a bench at the end of a path, a water feature, an architectural tree or shrub, a topiary shape, a statue or a sculpture. Focal points give the garden cohesion and add to the bare bones during the winter when many plants have died down.

A PATH CAN ALSO BE used as a 'desire line' — the way that is automatically taken across a garden to lead to a feature. In front gardens the 'desire line' is often the short cut the postman takes across the lawn. Desire lines like this are important — often the shortest route is the best and can be incorporated into the design in some way, such as making

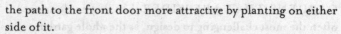

the path to the front door more attractive by planting on either side of it.

Paths need to be a minimum of 1.2 metres wide: this gives enough space to accommodate a wheelbarrow or two people walking side by side. The way you lay paths will affect the mood of the garden: narrow and straight paths are 'fast' while wider, more meandering paths slow the pace.

TOP TIP

When planning patios or decks, remember to leave enough space for a table and a few chairs — you'll need a minimum of 2.4 metres square.

MEAN BORDERS DON'T WORK. Allow a generous area for growing plants. They need space, and that means 1.5 or even 2 metres from front to back. Anything less means you will only be able to plant single plants — you won't achieve any decent depth or combinations, and shrubs and perennials will either spill over a lawn and kill the edges or obstruct a path and need constant cutting back.

CRISP EDGES to paths, borders and lawns give a smart finish and go a long way towards making a garden look well designed. Lengths of timber sunk a couple of centimetres into the ground ensure that the lawn does not creep into the border; they also help mowing, saving hours of work with a pair of edging shears. Paths edged with a contrasting brick, or gravel paths edged with brick, define areas and, in winter, when the garden has died down, add greatly to the overall design.

SEATING AUTOMATICALLY CREATES a feeling of relaxation, so add plenty of these areas, even if they have room for only one seat. The direction in which the sun rises or sets is crucial to the positioning of seating areas. Most people don't sit in the garden until they come home from work, so the best place for a seat may be somewhere where you can view the sunset. In addition, you may want a table and chairs to catch the morning sun for weekend breakfasts. Or you may prefer to sit in shade. Whatever your preference, you need to know where the sun is coming from. Then consider what you might plant next to your seats — the 'evening' area, for example, cries out for plants that release their perfume at that time of day.

EVERY GARDEN HAS CORNERS and it is important to consider how each one is used — for a seating area, a shady or sunny planting scheme, a children's garden, a focal point or just somewhere to place the shed. It is surprising how many themes corners can have: they can be the making of a well-designed garden.

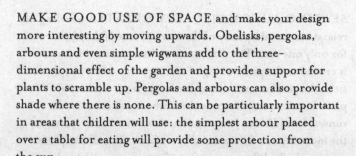

MAKE GOOD USE OF SPACE and make your design more interesting by moving upwards. Obelisks, pergolas, arbours and even simple wigwams add to the three-dimensional effect of the garden and provide a support for plants to scramble up. Pergolas and arbours can also provide shade where there is none. This can be particularly important in areas that children will use: the simplest arbour placed over a table for eating will provide some protection from the sun.

WHEN CHOOSING MATERIALS for hard areas, don't forget the 'less is more' dictum. Too many different-coloured paving slabs or bricks make a garden feel 'bitty'. Sticking to a few materials will give the garden a sense of unity.

GRAVEL CAN BE AN ECONOMICAL and low-maintenance answer to the problem of large planting areas. Cover the levelled space with landscape fabric and make slits in it so that you can plant through it. Then cover the fabric with a 5–7.5 cm layer of gravel. The gravel acts as a mulch, keeping watering to a minimum. Plants seed well in gravel, though, so you will still have to do some weeding.

> ### TOP TIP
> *Hiding eyesores like sheds, utility areas*
> *and compost bins is easy with a couple*
> *of trellis panels planted with a selection*
> *of climbers that provide foliage and flowers*
> *at different seasons.*

SLATE GIVES A DIFFERENT LOOK. It's a good alternative to gravel and can be used in exactly the same way, though it is more expensive.

WHEN YOU HAVE FINISHED PLANNING, you are ready to put your design into action. Before starting work, always mark out a design with rope, orange twine or even a garden hose to give an idea of how it will look. At this stage you can still adjust measurements and make areas larger or smaller. Don't worry about following hard and fast rules here. Remember that you are designing this garden for *you*, so if it feels right then it usually is right.

IN A NEW HOME WITH AN EXISTING GARDEN, it is advisable to wait a year to see what plants come through over the seasons before doing anything radical. Remove any you dislike, keep those you like, ask around or check reference books to help with identification and read up on how to care for them.

DESIGNING WITH PLANTS

Right plant right place is the mantra for planting in every garden. A plant will thrive if its needs are met. Most failures in gardening happen when plants are asked to grow where they don't want to. It is pointless to plant a sun-lover in shade and vice versa. Look to nature for the answer. In a shaded garden woodland plants will thrive, but don't expect them to grow in full sun. If you live on the coast, look around in other local gardens to see what plants are growing well — these will be the ones that can cope with the sandy soils and exposure to wind that are an inevitable part of this location.

IN MOST GARDENS there will be a spot that is sunny for some part of the day; there may also be a part that is always in the sun or always in shade. There may be some dappled shade and there may be a particularly damp area. Get to know your garden and its soil before choosing plants for each place. Dry shade under shrubs and trees and dry soil by house walls can be difficult places to fill with plants, but rest assured that there are plants to suit every aspect and every soil.

> ## TOP TIP
> *Remember, nature abhors a vacuum and will always fill an empty bit of soil. It is better to fill that space with a decorative plant before nature does it with a weed.*

SOIL TYPE IS CRUCIAL to what plants will grow. A simple soil test will tell you whether the soil is neutral, which means that most plants will grow; acid, which means that lime-hating plants like rhododendrons and azaleas will grow, but pinks won't; or alkaline, where the reverse will apply.

TEXTURE IS ANOTHER KEY FEATURE: you often read that certain plants like free-draining soil, for example. Test the texture of your soil by grabbing a handful and rolling it up into a ball. If it crumbles easily and does not bind together, then it is light and free-draining. If it sticks together and can be moulded into shapes, then it is most likely to be a heavy clay and will need the addition of lots of grit and compost to make it workable. Light soils do not hold water or nutrients very well, so may need additional compost or manure, but they warm up quickly in the spring. This allows

you to sow seeds and put plants in the ground earlier than
with heavy soils, which remain colder and possibly waterlogged
for longer. On the other hand, heavy soils are often richer
in nutrients. There are, of course, soils that are between these
two extremes and again it is worth getting to know what you
have in your garden.

WHEN DESIGNING WITH PLANTS there are a few
key things to remember:

Repetition. Use the same plant more than once to carry the
eye along a border and through a garden.

Grouping. Use more than one plant to make a bold group.
Plant in threes, fives or sevens. When gardening on a budget,
buy one decent-sized plant and divide it before planting it out.

Simplicity. Keep planting designs simple. Don't throw
everything together unless it is for a cottage-garden effect. To
get a 'designed' look in a small space, use only a few different
plants, but use them in quantity. And limit the colour range.

Spacing. Don't plant too close together. Always check the likely
spread of your plant as well as its height. A small plant put in
the ground in spring will often treble its size by mid-summer.

Placing. Experiment by positioning plants in their pots before
putting them in the ground. That way you can move them
around and adjust them to get the best look.

TOP TIP

*If you want to put a bench or seat around a tree, make
sure you leave enough room for the trunk to expand.*

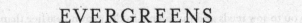

EVERGREENS

Evergreen plants can form a large part of the garden's structure, especially in winter.

Evergreens for structure

Topiary shapes like box balls can act as full stops at the edges of borders or placed in pots. They can add unity to a chaotic planting scheme and will still be around in winter when everything else has died down.

Hebes (*Hebe* spp.) come in many varieties with good strong leaves and form as well as flowers in late summer.

Mexican orange blossom (*Choisya* spp.) is another good evergreen, giving structure to the garden as well as having perfumed flowers and aromatic foliage.

Yew (*Taxus* spp.) requires patience — it may take five years for a decent hedge to develop. But once this happens, it forms the perfect backdrop for plants.

CHAPTER THREE – DESIGN

Small columnar trees like juniper (*Juniperus* spp.) or Italian cypress (*Cupressus sempervirens)* are invaluable for 'Mediterranean' planting schemes, especially when repeated along a border.

Evergreen viburnums such as *Viburnum davidii* are perfect for winter when most perennials are dormant.

Bamboos (*Phyllostachys* spp.) add movement, sound and height and can be used to hide eyesores or fill unpromising corners.

Palms such as *Cordyline australis* and *Cycas revoluta* are perfect plants for 'tropical' schemes, adding a touch of the exotic and backbone to your planting. Many of them are hardy in our climate, but always check with the garden centre or nursery.

EVERGREENS HAVE MANY DESIGN USES.

They can be planted as focal points or to define the end of a border. Box balls can be placed uniformly along the edge of a border to draw the eye along it. Columnar yews or juniper may be positioned so that they can be viewed from a window or door, or you could put two together to form a 'gateway' into another part of the garden. Bamboos may act as a screen or a green backdrop to a statue or sculpture and perfumed evergreens like the Mexican orange blossom can be delightful placed along a path where there is frequent traffic.

TOPIARY IS A GREAT WAY of turning evergreens into garden 'features'. Clipping topiary shapes needs nothing more than a pair of sharp shears and a fairly good eye. Clip less rather than more and keep reducing the size until you form a good, tight shape. Clip from early June (Derby Day is the traditional time) to the middle of September – but no later, because any pruning encourages soft new growth which, if you clip too late, will be killed by early frosts, turn brown and damage the plant.

> ## A BIT OF TOPIARY HISTORY
>
> The art of clipping trees or shrubs into decorative shapes goes
> back thousands of years to the Egyptian and Persian cultures,
> where formal gardens were created with paths, fountains, planters,
> borders and neatly clipped hedges and shrubs. The concept
> reached Rome about 2000 years ago and survived into the Middle
> Ages, thanks to monks who kept it alive in the cloisters of their
> monasteries. During the Renaissance the idea spread through
> Europe, reaching its zenith in the tightly clipped hedges of the
> formal gardens at Versailles and the massive parterres, clipped
> hedges and topiary shapes that were fashionable in Tudor England.

CLIMBERS

These are some of the most useful plants in the garden, giving
interest and colour all year round and providing scent and
shelter for birds. There are climbers that will cover all areas
of the garden, and all aspects from sun to shade.

Climbers for sun

Jasmine (*Jasminum officinalis*) has glossy leaves and a heady,
evocative scent. For abundant flowers do not plant in soil that
is too rich. Place in a sunny spot such as up a trellis at the edge
of a patio.

Roses (*Rosa* spp. – see page 28 for recommended varieties)
can quickly cover unsightly fences and arbours and are
invaluable in cottage garden and classic schemes. Plant
in rich, well-manured soil.

Annual climbers such as morning glory (*Ipomoea purpurea*), Spanish flag (*Ipomoea lobata*) and sweet peas (*Lathyrus odoratus*) are easy and cheap to grow from seed and can quickly cover an obelisk or wigwam. Sow indoors in early spring and plant out in May.

Honeysuckle (*Lonicera* spp.) covers fences, walls and trellis quickly and can fill a garden with evening fragrance. Plant *L*. 'Belgica' for late spring flowers and *L. periclymenum* for summer perfume.

Passion flower (*Passiflora caerulea*) is a vigorous climber for covering sheds and romping up fences and trellis. It erupts into flower in mid-summer and carries on until late autumn, often producing large yellow fruits (not very edible) in a long, hot summer.

Star jasmine (*Trachelospermum jasminoides*) has evergreen leaves and very fragrant jasmine-like flowers in summer. A bit tender, but excellent for sheltered warm walls or small courtyard gardens.

TOP TIP

Planting a climber at an angle towards its support will encourage it to grow towards the support. It will also prevent the roots from being too sheltered and away from rain.

Climbers for shade

Climbing hydrangea (*Hydrangea petiolaris*) is self-clinging and perfect for north walls. Slow to get going, once established it will produce flat white flower heads in summer.

Ivy (*Hedera helix*). If all else fails grow ivy. It is particularly good for dry shade, where challenging growing conditions will put a check on a too-vigorous growth habit. It's good for wildlife, too.

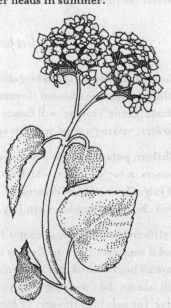

Chocolate vine (*Akebia quinata*) is a very quick-growing climber that can cover a large space like a pergola or north wall in no time. Chocolate-scented flowers are produced in spring.

Clematis **'Alba Luxurians'.** There are a few clematis that will grow in shade, but a white-flowered variety such as this creates light where none exists.

—— WALL SHRUBS ——

Shrubs which lend themselves to growing against warm walls, where their natural leggy habit can be trained and tied in, really broaden the palette of plants that will cover fences, walls and pergolas and act as a framework for other, more delicate climbers such as clematis. With a little forethought, a 'double whammy' of flowering can be achieved: if, for example, a wall shrub flowers in late spring and early summer, you could plant a clematis that flowers later on in the summer alongside it to extend the flowering season.

Perfect partners

Pineapple broom (*Cytisus battandieri*) flowers in summer with yellow, pineapple-scented flowers and silver leaves. *Clematis viticella* 'Etoile Violette' will flower in late summer with purple flowers, making a good contrast against the broom's leaves.

Chilean potato tree (*Solanum crispum* 'Glasnevin') has violet flowers in early summer which often continue until the end of July. *Clematis texensis* 'Princess of Wales', with elegant, dark pink, bell flowers, blooms in July through to September.

Californian lilac (*Ceanothus* spp.) has dark green glossy leaves and is smothered in blue flowers in May. By June the flowers have all but finished, but the annual climber morning glory will take on the flowering in July: try *Ipomoea tricolor* 'Heavenly Blue' for pale blue flowers, or *Ipomoea purpurea* for dark purple.

CLEMATIS

Clematis belong to the Ranunculaceae, the same family as anemones, buttercups and hardy geraniums. There are over 400 types to choose from and they are the perfect climber for most gardens; most don't take up much space and, while some will use other plants as a host to scramble up, lots are happy to grow up trellis, walls and fences once adequate support has

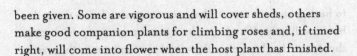

been given. Some are vigorous and will cover sheds, others make good companion plants for climbing roses and, if timed right, will come into flower when the host plant has finished.

PLANTING CLEMATIS CORRECTLY is crucial to their success. They need their roots in shade and their heads in the sun, so choose their position carefully. They are also hungry plants and need soil to be well prepared, with lots of compost and manure added. Water the pot thoroughly before planting and then dig a hole twice as wide as the pot and at least 15 cm deeper. If planting next to a wall, fence or host climber, make sure the clematis is at least 60 cm away. Remove the plant from the pot and loosen the roots slightly before placing in the hole, refilling with the soil/compost mixture and firming in. Finally add a thick mulch of compost or stones to keep the roots cool and moist.

CLEMATIS WILT is one of the most annoying diseases of all, as the plant will be growing happily and then, overnight, it will collapse and turn black. The die-back starts at the tip of a shoot or a leaf and spreads downwards to the base of the plant. Some large-flowered types seem to be particularly susceptible, while small-flowered varieties may be totally unaffected. The disease is caused by a fungus whose spores are produced from tiny fruiting bodies on infected stems and spread by water splash. The fungus can remain in the soil in old, infected plant material. There is no cure, but cutting back the wilted shoots

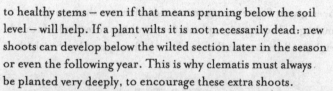

to healthy stems – even if that means pruning below the soil level – will help. If a plant wilts it is not necessarily dead: new shoots can develop below the wilted section later in the season or even the following year. This is why clematis must always be planted very deeply, to encourage these extra shoots.

Clematis which are generally trouble free are the species types, which include *C. montana, armandii, alpina, macropetala, viticella, texensis* and *tangutica.*

HARD PRUNE ALL NEWLY PLANTED CLEMATIS

within the first year of planting to encourage a strong root system and new shoots from below the soil level. Thereafter, for pruning purposes, clematis are divided into three groups:

Group 1 are the small-flowered species which flower in early spring on the growth they made the previous year. Remove dead and damaged stems and generally reduce the size of the plant to fit the space immediately after it has flowered. To renovate the plant completely if it becomes too twiggy or woody or stops flowering well, cut down to within 15–30 cm of the base.

Group 2 produce large flowers in May and June on short stems from the previous year's growth, or later on the current season's growth. Remove dead and damaged stems before growth starts in the early spring and trim remaining stems to just above a pair of strong buds.

Group 3 flower in late summer and may be large-flowering, smaller-flowering or herbaceous types, but all flower on growth made in the current year. In early spring, before new growth begins, cut back all the growth to a strong pair of buds 15 cm above soil level.

CLEMATIS FOR BIG AREAS

Clematis montana and all its varieties flower in May and are very vigorous, often covering outbuildings, sheds and pergolas. Cut back after flowering only if the plant gets out of hand.

Clematis tangutica and its varieties flower later in the summer with yellow, 'orange peel'-like, round bell flowers followed by fluffy seed heads which persist on the plant throughout winter. *C.* 'Bill MacKenzie' is a variety of *tangutica* but has larger flowers.

-CLEMATIS FOR SPRING AND SUMMER-

Clematis alpina 'Frances Rivis' is one of the first of the year and is a perfect plant for a trellis, often smothered in pale blue double bells of flowers. Cut back only if the plant grows out of its allotted space and then only after flowering.

Clematis armandii loves to grow in a sunny and sheltered spot, but once it is happy it will be vigorous, evergreen and, in early spring, covered with superb white, sweetly scented flowers.

Varieties of *Clematis texensis* and *C. viticella* mostly flower from July to September, though some will still be going strong in October. They scramble over trees, trellis and other climbers and come in a range of colours.

DESIGNING A BORDER

Always start with the aspect — whether it is in sun or shade or a bit of both — and research the plants that will thrive there. Then consider what the backbone of the scheme is going to be — is it a tree, a shrub or a climber going up an obelisk? Think of the backdrop — is it a hedge or a fence that needs to be covered with climbers? And if you want the area to have interest for as long as possible, choose plants that have a long flowering time or a mixture of seasonal flowering plants.

PLACING AND PLANTING. The rule of thumb is to have the tallest at the back and the shortest at the front. Position trees, shrubs and climbers first of all, then perennials and ground cover, and finally fill the gaps with bulbs. Remember that, if you are planting in spring, most perennials will grow at least three times larger than they are in the pot, so allow enough space in between. Water all the plants in well and add a mulch to retain moisture and give a good 'finish'. Water new plantings every couple of days to help them get established.

PLANTS FOR SUN

Plants have evolved and adapted themselves to different environments and plants which thrive in hot and dry conditions tend to have:

tough leathery leaves

grey or silver leaves which reflect light

hairy leaves which reduce water loss and often give a grey or silver colour to the leaf

fleshy leaves that hold water (these are known as succulents)

Good plants for sun:

Sedums (*Sedum* spp.) flower late in the summer with flat, pink flower heads and are major attractants of butterflies. Cut back to the ground in spring.

Blue mist (*Caryopteris* x *clandonensis*) has blue flowers and silver leaves which are aromatic when crushed. Cut the shrub back in late spring to about 30 cm.

Zonal pelargoniums (*Pelargonium* spp.) add bright splashes of colour and thrive on neglect. Plant in gritty soils and water occasionally during summer. In containers, they should not be allowed to dry out completely — water when the top of the compost is dry.

Lavender (*Lavandula* spp.) is the perfect plant for lining sunny paths, whether in the border or in pots. Harvest in summer and never cut the plant back into old wood as it will not rejuvenate. Take cuttings regularly for fresh plants.

Russian sage (*Perovskia* spp.) produces a dark blue haze of flowers atop silvery foliage. This plant thrives on neglect, needing only to be pruned back to about 30 cm in spring.

Wormwood (*Artemisia*) provides valuable ground cover for the driest of places and is ideal for edging borders. Trim back in spring for fresh new growth.

PLANTS FOR SHADE

Again, look to nature for clues to what plants will grow well in shade. In the spring, before the leaves appear on the trees, bulbs and bluebells carpet the woodland floor. As the leaves break open and the canopy closes over, another layer of plants appears, covering the ground. Somewhere in the middle are young saplings and shrubs. You can recreate this effect in your own garden by planting shady spots in layers.

Bulbs for shade

Blues, whites and yellows show up better in shade, so go for **daffodils**, ***Anemone blanda***, **scillas**, **snowdrops** and **cyclamen**.

Ground cover for shade

Lady's mantle (*Alchemilla mollis*) has green hairy leaves that hang on to water droplets and lime-green froths of flowers that light up shady areas.

Lungworts (*Pulmonaria* spp.) have green leaves with white spots and flower very early in the year, giving valuable spring colour.

Ferns such as *Asplenium* and *Dryopteris* spp. are the perfect foliage plant, elegant as they unfurl in spring and then covering even the driest shade with their fronds.

Dead nettle (*Lamium maculatum*) spreads and creeps along the ground, its green and white foliage adding light under shrubs and trees.

Foam flower (*Tiarella cordifolia*) has clumps of foliage topped by small white flowers, the foliage persisting from early spring throughout the summer and into autumn.

Flowers for shade

Japanese anemones (*Anemone japonica*). Many woodland flowers are over by the summer but Japanese anemones, with their white flowers with bright yellow centres, appear in late summer and carry on into autumn.

Solomon's seal (*Polygonatum*) has arching stems and flowers that dangle from underneath in late spring.

Hellebores (*Helleborus* spp.) provide the showiest flowers in the early winter (see page 62, for more details).

Bleeding heart (*Dicentra spectabilis*) is another late-spring flower; it dangles down from arching stems, dying back for the summer.

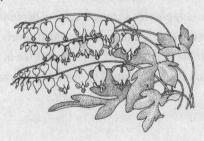

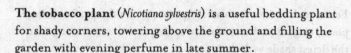

The tobacco plant (*Nicotiana sylvestris*) is a useful bedding plant for shady corners, towering above the ground and filling the garden with evening perfume in late summer.

Granny's bonnets (*Aquilegia* spp.) are good border plants for dappled shade and ideal for shady spots in cottage gardens.

Foxgloves (*Digitalis* spp.) are the archetypal plant for any shady spot although they will also grow in sun and the white varieties particularly stand out.

Shrubs for shade

Camellias (*Camellia* spp.) are the show-stoppers of the late-winter garden. Being plants that thrive on the edge of woodland, some will flower from February through until May. They are also good in pots.

Japanese quince (*Chaenomeles*) are good to train against shady walls and give colour when not much is around in early spring.

Japanese maples (*Acer palmatum*) thrive in dappled shade out of the wind and have elegant leaves, attractive form and brilliant autumn colour. They are good in pots in shady, sheltered positions.

> **TOP TIP**
> *All newly planted shrubs, trees and perennials*
> *will need regular watering, particularly*
> *those in shady spots as they are often in*
> *'rain shadows' caused by overhanging trees*
> *or by fences or walls.*

GOOD-VALUE PERENNIALS

It isn't easy to achieve continuous colour all year round, but in small gardens it is possible to choose a few 'good achievers' or 'value for money' perennials that will flower for a long time over the summer with little attention apart from dead-heading and occasional cutting back.

Penstemons (*Penstemon* spp.) flower continuously throughout summer into autumn and are fairly trouble free. Cut back to new growth in late spring.

Masterwort (*Astrantia major*) will grow in sun or dappled shade, flowering for a long time from early to late summer. Cut back to the ground after the first flush of flowers and fresh foliage and flowers will appear and continue into autumn.

Geranium psilostemon is a large geranium, up to 90 cm in height with large leaves and magenta flowers. Cut back in July and it will flower again until late autumn. It seeds around freely, growing in dappled shade and in sun. *Geranium* 'Rozanne' has tough leaves and pale blue flowers needing no attention. It will grow in sun or shade, flowers continuously and even thrives in a hanging basket.

Violas (*Viola* spp.) are perfect edgers for borders and fill pots. They can flower themselves to death and need to be sheared to the ground occasionally to keep them going.

Salvia **'Mainacht'** has blue spikes that will keep on coming if it is continuously dead-headed.

CHAPTER THREE – BORDERS

DESIGNING WITH COLOUR

Every colour is affected by the colours around it and so colour combinations are important in design. Contrasting colours, such as blue and yellow, highlight the differences between them and intensify the brightness of each. Harmonizing colours, such as purples and reds, are more subtle. Hot colours — reds, oranges and yellows, the colours of fire — are exciting and intense and need sun if they are to sizzle. Cool blues, greens and whites are restful and soothing. Plant them in the areas where you want to sit and relax.

Every colour produces a reaction in us:

Green is vital to life and indicates water and vegetation in abundance, which has a reassuring effect. It is in the centre of the colour spectrum and represents perfect balance. In the garden, green is the constant foil to all other colours.

White is not really a colour; it is the effect created when all the colours of the spectrum are reflected. White glows in the evening when other colours recede.

Blue is rarely found in nature but is deemed to lower blood pressure, be soothing and calming and encourage reflection. It absorbs less light than other colours, so blue plants always appear further away than they are.

Cool pale pink is restful to the eye and brain, but a hot magenta pink has a stimulating effect. Pale pinks combined with white or blue are cool; magenta with purple is sophisticated and subtle; dark pinks and orange sizzle.

Red is a passionate colour which attracts attention and creates drama. It stimulates the body, creating a rise in temperature and blood pressure. It is used in 'hot' schemes but can be wonderfully subtle when combined with dark red, bronze, purple or coppery foliage.

Yellow reflects more light than any other colour. It raises the spirits and is bright and cheerful; full of sunshine, it's the colour most associated with spring.

TOP TIP
Bright light washes out the cool colours, so blues, greens and purples are better suited to shaded areas.

THE JOY OF DESIGN is that no two gardens will be the same. What you do with your garden is purely down to your individual taste, so whether it is a jungle garden, formal, informal, cottage style or full of regimented rows of vegetables or bedding, it is what pleases you that matters.

THE JOY OF GARDENING is that nobody gets it right first time. Or even second time. It is absolutely fine to constantly move plants, replant areas and tinker with colour schemes. Nowhere in the garden is ever going to be absolutely perfect and, if it is, the perfection is momentary. But throughout the gardening year there are sometimes quite a few of those moments. It's the reason gardeners garden.

CHAPTER FOUR

POTS

*Being portable, containers are ideal for anyone planning
to move house and, if you are a compulsive re-arranger,
containers allow you to reinvent your surroundings without
the bother of digging everything up.*

ALAN TITCHMARSH
How to be a Gardener

GARDENING IN CONTAINERS

One of the main attractions of container gardening is its versatility.
You can plant almost anything in a pot and use almost any vessel
as a container, to produce an infinite range of possibilities
for your patio.

RICHARD ROSENFELD
Containers for Patios

You can grow almost anything in a pot, but the key thing to remember is that it won't survive on its own. Putting a plant in a container removes it from its natural environment and makes it totally dependent on you for water and food.

A container can be anything from an old bucket to a window box, hanging basket or wooden trough. It doesn't matter what form it takes, as long as it can hold enough compost to support the plant and has drainage holes for water to escape.

BECAUSE TERRACOTTA IS SO POROUS it will absorb water, which means that a plant in a terracotta pot will need more frequent watering – it will dry out a lot quicker than a plant in a ceramic or plastic container. If you want to conserve water it is a good idea, therefore, before planting, to line the pot with plastic or an empty compost bag with holes punched into the bottom. This will keep the soil moist for longer. Alternatively, soak a terracotta pot for a few hours before planting it up.

A POTTED HISTORY OF POTS

The earliest representation of a pot-grown plant can be found in Malta at the temple of Hagar Qim, which dates from 3150–2500 BC. In ancient Egypt, Ramses III (1182–1151 BC) was a great builder of temples and palaces who also established over 500 semi-public gardens, growing papyrus, flowers and shrubs in pots which were placed along the walkways. The Greeks learned the art of container gardening from the Egyptians and grew herbs and vegetables, and then the Romans took pot-growing into their urban environments, using them to brighten up window-sills, roofs and balconies.

Medieval pots were made of earthenware, painted metal, wattle or terracotta. Later came stone, lead and wooden tubs. The mass-produced clay pot didn't enter the scene until 1860, with the invention of the turning mould machine. Terracotta, which means 'cooked earth', has been used throughout history. It is much lighter than many other materials used for pots, is long lasting and can tolerate very low winter temperatures. The red clay that makes terracotta flowerpots must be fired at a low temperature, which keeps it porous. It breathes, so the plants' roots can breathe. The traditional funnel shape makes repotting easier and ushers water rapidly from top to bottom, so the roots don't wallow in water.

Long Toms, which are funnel-shaped but taller, were put into service in the nineteenth century for plants whose roots plunge straight down, like rosemary. Wide, shallow containers catered to begonias, azaleas and other plants with roots that travel horizontally; and little terracotta thumbs or thimbles acted as starter pots for new transplants. All containers had drainage holes, which were sometimes raised off the ground by a small pedestal built into the pot, to prevent worms from gaining entry.

SOIL FOR CONTAINERS

Bearing in mind that, by growing a plant in a pot, you have put it in an artificial environment, you must reflect its needs in your choice of compost.

JOHN INNES COMPOSTS are a range of composts developed at the John Innes Institute, which was named after a nineteenth-century London property dealer who left his fortune to horticultural research.

Based mainly on loam rather than peat, there are several formulae for the different types of John Innes composts. They mix loam, peat, sand and fertilizer in varying proportions, depending on what the compost is going to be used for, from sowing seeds to planting established shrubs.

HISTORICALLY, PEAT has been chosen as a key ingredient of 'potting compost' because of its water and nutrient retention. However, we now know that peat will regenerate itself at a rate of only 5 mm a year and the extraction rate is significantly higher than that, so it is not an eco-friendly material to use.

At Berryfields we have not grown plants in peat for years. We don't need peat for 90 per cent of what we grow, and there are many good alternatives: peat-free composts have come on by leaps and bounds recently and there are some really good products on the market.

PEAT-BASED PRODUCTS tend to hold moisture, but once peat has dried out it is extremely difficult to rewet. Traditionally gardeners have been taught to soak pots on a daily basis to prevent this from happening.

PEAT-FREE COMPOST does not dry out so quickly and even if it does it is easy to re-wet. Don't overwater plants in peat-free compost, particularly seedlings, or they may rot off.

PEAT-FREE COMPOSTS give a real boost of feed to plants initially, but after about six weeks nutrients are rapidly depleted. Once plants have gone past the seedling stage and have been potted on, then a comfrey feed (see page 129) is beneficial.

BERRYFIELDS POTTING COMPOST RECIPES

Seed

When creating a mix in which seeds will germinate, structure is important. The compost does not need to be full of nutrients, but should have a fine, open texture.
We use:
2 parts leaf mould
1 part sieved loam
1 part garden compost
1 part sand or fine-grade grit

Pricking out

Seedlings need the extra boost of a more nutrient-based compost:
1 part garden compost
1 part loam
1 part leaf mould
1 part sand or grit

Potting

Long-term potting mixtures should carry a lot of nutrients to help the plant over the course of its life:
2 parts sieved garden compost
1 part leaf mould
1 part loam
1 part sand or grit

POTS FOR SUN

*Container, plants, situation — good design involves arranging
these three features so that an attractive visual impact is coupled
with good growing conditions for the plants. This rarely happens
by accident — the secret is careful planning.*

DR D G HESSAYON
The Container Expert

Most plants that thrive in a sunny situation are those that,
in their natural environment, grow in very free-draining
soil, so add extra grit to their potting compost.

Good plants for pots in sun

Pelargoniums (*Pelargonium* spp.) need very little care —
a sunny spot, good gritty compost and regular dead-heading
will guarantee flowers all summer until the first frosts.
Their stems are thick and store water, so they are great for
sun. At the end of summer, take cuttings and overwinter
them indoors.

Lavender (*Lavandula* spp.) is the perfect plant for pots (see
Herbs, page 128), thriving in sun and just needing to be cut
back in the late summer after the flowers have been harvested
for lavender bags and pot pourri.

Tender succulents such as *Echeveria* thrive on neglect and
can safely be left for the holiday period because their thick
leaves store water. They multiply quickly and 'baby' succulents
can be pulled from the base of the mother plant and potted
up in gritty compost. These plants will not survive outside
in the winter months so keep them on a window-sill indoors.

Herbs (see page 172) grow particularly well in pots and are ideal to place outside the kitchen door for instant culinary use!

POTS FOR SHADE

Shady areas of the garden can be transformed by a collection of pots filled with plants that don't crave a lot of sun. To keep them happy, replicate a woodland floor by adding leaf mould or composted bark to ordinary peat-free compost.

Good plants for pots in shade

Ferns unfurl in early spring and come in a range of leaf textures from shiny to deeply divided. Most keep their leaves until late winter, when they will turn brown. Cut down this foliage in early spring to allow new growth to come through.

Spring bulbs make the most of whatever sun may be available and will flower in all but the densest shade. Plant up pots of snowdrops and miniature daffodils for instant spring colour.

Box (*Buxus* spp.) adds structure when trained into topiary shapes (see page 146) and makes a good centrepiece for a potted scheme of perhaps ferns and bulbs.

> ### TOP TIP
> *A good trick for potting on is to put your smaller pot inside the larger one, fill around it with compost and tap your plant out to fit perfectly into the hole you've created.*

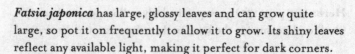

Fatsia japonica has large, glossy leaves and can grow quite large, so pot it on frequently to allow it to grow. Its shiny leaves reflect any available light, making it perfect for dark corners.

Hostas are often better grown in pots because, in the open ground, they are very susceptible to slug attack. Grow them in a ceramic container so the slugs can't climb up and get at them. Some hostas have variegated margins to the leaves and it is these varieties that look best in shade.

PRODUCE IN POTS

Every location offers an opportunity for planting, so be inventive and make good use of the space that is available. Hang baskets from brackets on walls, place pots on stairs, and on front doorsteps, and position boxes on window-ledges.

GAY SEARCH
Gardening without a Garden

FRUIT

STRAWBERRIES If you have too little space to let strawberries run riot, you can grow them in pots. About three plants to a large pot should ensure a decent crop without letting them get crowded. For earlier fruit take the pot into a conservatory or greenhouse in February and the plant will start to grow and therefore fruit earlier than if it had been left outside. But remember to take the pot outside again once fruiting is over, as strawberries need the cold of winter to produce flowers and fruit for the following year.

FRUIT TREES Permanent container-grown fruit
trees need more regular attention than their open-ground
counterparts, particularly with regard to watering and
fertilizing, since their roots are obviously more contained
and prone to drying out. A peat-free, soil-based compost is
an ideal growing medium as the weight of the soil gives the pot
stability. The choice of the container itself is also important
– the heavier the pot, the more stable it is, making terracotta
ideal. Do not, however, plant a small tree in a very large pot
at the outset as this will affect its growth and fruiting.

Fruit trees may eventually become pot-bound and will
need repotting into larger containers every two years until they
reach full size: do this when the tree is dormant and the leaves
have fallen off. With early-flowering fruit trees, such as
peaches, being able to move them in or out of cover to avoid
frosts and provide ideal temperatures also helps to ensure the
best possible crop. Cover with a horticultural fleece at night
for added protection.

HERBS AND SPICES

Herbs that thrive in pots include basil, chives, coriander, oregano, parsley, rosemary and sage

TO PLANT HERBS IN CONTAINERS, first cover the base of the pot with old crocks, stones or grit. This mimics the Mediterranean conditions the herbs would grow in. Then add lots of grit to the compost. Fill the pot two-thirds full with compost. Gently tap each herb out of its original pot and sit it in the larger container so that the top of the rootball comes 2–3 cm short of the rim. It's important not to overfill the pot with herbs; this can stress the plants and impair their growth. About three pots of herbs to a large container is ideal. Top up with compost, firm gently and water well.

HERBS ARE MORE LIKELY to dry out in pots as there is less soil to hold water, so in the summer watering daily either in the morning or in the evening may be necessary. Although herbs love warmth and light, full sun all day may cause them to wilt or run to seed, so remove any flowers immediately (after all, the leaves are what you are growing them for) and move the pots into a bit of shade now and again. Give them an organic seaweed feed once a week to top up the nutrient levels in the compost.

CHILLIES IN POTS

All peppers love the heat and need a fairly long season to grow from seed to fruit, so sow seeds in a cell tray in mid March to give them enough time to develop before days and nights start to cool at the end of summer. Fill the tray with compost and water it, allowing it to drain for a few minutes before dropping

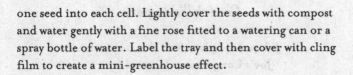

one seed into each cell. Lightly cover the seeds with compost and water gently with a fine rose fitted to a watering can or a spray bottle of water. Label the tray and then cover with cling film to create a mini-greenhouse effect.

CHILLI SEEDS need warmth – about 26–29°C, to begin the germination process – but light is not critical at this stage. An electric seed propagator is the ideal starting ground, but an airing cupboard will do. Keep the compost moist but not soggy, as overwatering will damage seedlings and may stop the germination process altogether. Seeds generally germinate within two weeks but may take up to a month. As soon as they germinate they need bright light – keep them on a window-sill or in a conservatory or greenhouse, but move them away from the window-sill at night in case temperatures plummet.

Seedlings can be grown on at a temperature somewhat lower than that needed for germination (18–26°C) and when the seedlings are up and growing, and have at least two sets of leaves, it is less crucial that the compost is kept consistently moist. It is OK to let the top of the soil dry out, but check daily that the container has not dried out completely.

Prick out seedlings when they have several sets of leaves. Fill individual 7 cm pots with fresh compost, water lightly and leave to drain. Then make a well large enough to fit the contents of the seed cell. Carefully remove the plant from the cell, pushing up from the bottom. Try not to disturb the roots, as this may cause 'root shock'. Place the seedling into its new pot, gently firm and water lightly. Peppers will make new roots along their buried stems, so if your seedlings are spindly, cover them with soil up to the base of the bottom cluster of leaves.

Keep potting them on whenever the roots fill the pot. Once plants start to bear fruit, feed once or twice a week with a good all-purpose liquid fertilizer diluted to half strength.

Good chillies to grow

Jalapeño – green fruit that turn red
Joe's Long – extra-long red fruit
Habanero – very hot orange fruit
Hungarian Hot Wax – not too hot,
yellow fruit turning red
Cayenne – glossy red fruit

—AUBERGINES AND SWEET PEPPERS—

Like chillies, these are members of the potato family and with
a bit of know-how, are easy to grow in pots in a sunny spot.

Sow seed in cells or on the surface of a 7 cm pot, scattering
the seed thinly. Most of the seeds will germinate, so you don't
really need to allow for losses: two seeds per cell or pot are
plenty. Cover with a fine layer of vermiculite, water, label and
either place in a heated propagator or put a clear plastic bag
over the top, secure with a rubber band and position on a
warm and sunny window-sill. Seeds should germinate in about
a week. Remove the pot from the propagator or take off the
bag, place on a light window-sill and ensure the compost does
not dry out.

Pot on when seedlings are about 2 cm tall. Carefully loosen
the compost, then gently hold a leaf and lift, while levering
from beneath the roots with a dibber. Fill a 7-cm pot with
multi-purpose compost, level and tap to settle. Make a hole
in the centre of the compost with a dibber and lower in the
seedling until the leaves are just above the surface of the soil.
Gently firm in, water and label. Keep plants in a light place
and when roots show at the bottom of the pots, move into a
12 cm pot filled with multi-purpose compost. When plants are

about 20 cm tall, stake with a small cane or pea stick and secure with twine; when they reach about 30 cm, pinch out the growing tips to increase branching. Plants can go outside at the end of May or in June, as long as night-time temperatures do not dip below 10°C. Their final container should be a 5-litre pot.

Good aubergines to grow . . .

Violetta Lunga – long purple fruit
Red Egg – dumpy red fruit
Snowy – cylindrical white fruit
Moneymaker – glossy black fruit
Rosa Bianca – white and pink fruit

. . . and good sweet peppers

Big Banana – very long red fruit
Marconi Rosso – sweet, red, Italian heritage variety
Fiesta – shiny yellow fruit
Bell Boy – thick-skinned, green fruit
Purple Beauty – purple fruit that turn red when mature

Don't let aubergines or peppers dry out as this will result in a check in growth and loss of fruit. These are thirsty plants and on hot days may need watering in the morning and again in the evening. After the first flowers appear, feed once a week with a tomato fertilizer, liquid seaweed or comfrey. Between July and September fruits may be ready to harvest. Before the first frosts of autumn, cut down the plants completely and hang the branches indoors or in a shed, upside down with the fruit still on, so that it continues to ripen.

SALAD IN POTS

Young 'cut and come again' salad leaves are ideal for growing in containers and will also grow well in Gro-bags, wooden wine boxes, apple boxes and even fish boxes. Whatever the container, it should have a depth and width of at least 45 cm so that the compost does not dry out quickly and, like any pot intended for growing a plant, it should have drainage holes in the bottom.

SOW SUCCESSIONALLY, which means a pinch of seed every two weeks from the end of March to give continuous crops. Even with cut and come again lettuces a successional sowing ensures produce throughout the summer.

TOP TIP

When you go on holiday, dead-head all your container plants, place them in a child's paddling pool in a shady spot and put a couple of inches of water in the bottom.

Good veg for pots

Beetroot: the young leaves as well as the roots can be eaten.

Carrots: sow small and early carrots like Nantes or Amsterdam in February for June crops and, at the same time, Chanteney Red Cored, which produces smaller carrots. Sow a row every few weeks to maintain a good harvest.

Spinach and rocket: pick off the top leaves for salads and they will sprout again.

Salad onions: sow from February onwards.

Courgettes: a single plant in a large pot will spill over the sides and run along the ground, but it will still produce a good crop that should be picked regularly. The large leaves and bright yellow flowers are also attractive.

Climbing French and runner beans: put up a wigwam in a large, deep pot and sow directly into the compost, two seeds per cane, in early May.

Tomatoes are also good candidates for pot growing and their cultivation is no different than if they were grown in the open ground (see Food, page 100).

SHRUBS IN CONTAINERS

A shrub needs a good start if it is to spend its life in a container. As with all container-grown plants, you need to mimic the conditions in which it would naturally grow, and for shrubs that means a soil-based compost, which has more nutrients, is heavier and will drain better than a multi-purpose compost. Put crocks at the bottom of pots to prevent the drainage holes being clogged by compost and to keep the roots from being waterlogged in winter, when frozen water may expand and break the pot.

SHRUBS HAVE LARGE ROOT SYSTEMS that need lots of water even after heavy rain; in hot spells they may need watering twice a day, morning and evening. Any compost will only have enough nutrients to last a month to six weeks. Controlled-release fertilizers will feed a plant for about six months when it is in active growth. Most shrubs stop growing over winter and don't need feeding. In the spring remove the top 5–10 cm of compost and replace with fresh: this is a good time to add more nutrients. If the shrub has grown too big for its pot, take it out, tease out the roots and repot it in a slightly larger container, backfilling with fresh compost. Potting a plant on into a container that is much larger than its rootball may result in waterlogging and the plant may die.

POT PESTS

Whatever you grow in a pot, it is almost certain that, at some time, a garden pest will come along and start munching at something. Slugs and snails have an almost ninja-like ability to launch themselves into pots, window boxes and even hanging baskets! Copper tape around the rim of pots is an effective deterrent. Or you could choose ceramic-glazed pots, which slugs and snails can't slither up, but really vigilance is the key.

—— WHAT NOT TO WORRY ABOUT ——

Ants sometimes build nests and woodlice like to congregate under pots, but both of them are relatively harmless.

WOODLICE MAY FEED on soft plant growth like seedlings or strawberries and sometimes enlarge damage already done by slugs, but they do no other harm, spending the day in dark, damp places under pots, logs and low-growing plants and moving around at night looking for decaying vegetation, which is their main food source.

ANTS ARE MORE OF A NUISANCE than a destructive pest. They feed on insects, farming blackfly and greenfly for honeydew, but if you clean aphids and greenfly off plants regularly, then the ants will go. They may disturb the roots if they build their nests in pots, but they won't kill the plants.

—— WHAT TO WORRY ABOUT ——

In containers the main pest is the vine weevil grub, which particularly loves primulas, polyanthus, heucheras and sedum. The adult beetles feed on the foliage of plants and shrubs and are fond of rhododendrons, euonymus, hydrangeas and primulas – notches in the leaves are a tell-tale sign, so if you spot those, look out for beetles that are about 9 mm long with a pear-shaped body. They can be seen at night feeding on foliage, move slowly and can't fly. All the adults are female and lay hundreds of small brown eggs between April and September. These eventually hatch into fat, white grubs with pale brown heads. The grubs feed on the roots of plants, which will then just collapse overnight.

A torchlit foray into the garden on spring and summer evenings will often reap a harvest of vine weevils, and a daylight search under pots may also unveil a few culprits. Birds, frogs, toads and ground beetles eat them and a biological and chemical control is available which can be applied as soon as the soil warms up in spring and again in early September: this should deal with the grubs before they grow large enough to cause damage.

WINTER PROTECTION FOR CONTAINERS.

Container-grown plants are much more at risk from winter damage than plants growing in the border. They do not have the shelter of a snug blanket of soil over them and, even though plants in the soil do get frozen, those in pots – especially the less hardy varieties – are more vulnerable. Therefore the pots need to be wrapped with bubble wrap to keep the roots and the soil from freezing. Moving pots to a more sheltered spot by a south-facing wall also helps. Tender plants such as succulents, some herbs and tender perennials need to be brought into the house during the worst of the winter weather.

HANGING BASKETS

The main thing to know about hanging baskets is that they dry out very quickly and plants will need watering twice a day, dead-heading regularly and feeding once a week. A small basket will dry out even more quickly than a larger one.

LINERS ARE CRITICAL to the success of the planting and really help with moisture retention. Moss does not hold water well and is not very environmentally friendly; coconut fibre and other similar fabric liners are better, but by far the best is an old wool jumper (buy a cheap one from a charity shop if you haven't got anything suitable) cut to fit the basket and lined at the bottom with a piece of bin liner.

PLANT UP by balancing the basket on top of a bucket, put in the liner and then cover the bottom of the basket with soil to a depth of about 2.5 cm. Use a fairly light peat-free compost with some controlled-release fertilizer granules added. Cut three holes through the liner, then take a plant and gently feed the rootball through the existing hole in the side of the basket, lining up with a hole in the liner. Rest the roots on the soil and make sure all the rootball is inside the basket. Repeat this around the basket, eventually feeding plants from the outside through the three holes you made in the liner. Add another layer of compost, make another three holes in the liner and repeat the process until you reach the top of the basket. Then place plants evenly around the top of the basket, firming them in well. Water gently from the top and allow the basket to drain before hanging it up.

NEVER HANG OUT A HANGING BASKET until the end of May, as it is too cold at night and there is still a risk of a frost which will kill tender bedding plants.

HANGING BASKET
WATER-SAVING TIPS

Water with grey water – from cooking (e.g. boiled eggs),
the bath and washing-up water (it's all right to use water that
has had detergent in it as long as it is not greasy).

Use water from water butts.

Water in the early morning and again in the evening, when
less water will evaporate.

Put other pots underneath to be watered by the overflow.

Place ice cubes over the top of the compost: they will melt
and slowly water the basket. This ensures that the water does
not all just drain away, but is gradually absorbed by the soil.

Dunk dry hanging baskets in a bucket of water to ensure they
are fully wetted and there's less water waste.

Move baskets to a shadier spot on a really hot day to reduce
water loss.

Use cut-down plastic drinks bottles as funnels to direct water
into the basket. Place the neck of the bottle into the soil and then
water through the cut end. This will direct the water better and
ensure less waste as the water gradually drains into the basket.
The bottle can be hidden in the foliage at the top of the basket.

Good plants for hanging baskets in sun

Silvery-leaved trailing plants such as *Dicondra* survive drought well and do not need constant watering to survive

Pelargoniums (*Pelargonium* spp.) come in trailing varieties and, because they are adapted to survive sunny climates, will not need copious amounts of water.

Succulents (see Pots for Sun, page 168).

Trailing verbena (*Verbena* spp., including *Verbena x hybrida pendula*) come in a good variety of colours and flower for a long period of time from summer through to autumn.

Petunias (*Petunia x hybrida*) need regular dead-heading but will then give a blaze of colour and sometimes scent.

Good plants for hanging baskets in shade

Busy lizzies (*Impatiens* spp.) like moist soil and come in a huge array of bright colours.

Fuchsias (*Fuchsia* spp.). One fuchsia can fill a basket and will flower all summer and into autumn.

Begonias (*Begonia* spp.). One begonia corm started off on a windowsill in spring can be planted into a basket and will tumble down the sides.

Lobelia (*Lobelia* spp.) will flower in the sun but dry out quickly. Flowering is prolonged when they are grown in shade.

Creeping Jenny (*Lysimachia nummularia*) makes a good trailing plant and will spill down to the ground. The golden-leaved variety looks particularly good in shade.

BONSAI

BONSAI is the ancient art of miniaturizing trees by using a variety of cultivation techniques, such as shaping, watering and repotting in various types of container. A young sapling tree is the first requirement, preferably one with a slender stem and a few small branches. Hawthorn is a good choice in the UK, as it is suited to our climate. Large-leafed trees such as sycamore and horse chestnut are less suitable, although an oak can eventually become a spectacular large bonsai.

BONSAI WILL GROW INDOORS, but trees are best suited to growing outside, so it is best to plant it up into an ordinary pot in the garden until it is growing well. Bonsai can be planted up in the winter and kept indoors to stimulate it into growth but, as most trees are dormant in the winter, no real growth will happen until the spring.

ONCE THE TREE IS ACTIVELY GROWING, knock it out of its pot and inspect the roots. If there is a long tap root, trim back about a third of it to restrict the plant's growth. Remove any unwanted branches and shape others by trimming back to a bud, so that new branches will form and grow in the direction of that bud. Plant the tree into its permanent bonsai pot using a soil-based compost mixed with grit and sand to help with drainage. Make sure the pot has plenty of holes in the base to allow the water to drain away. Water in.

ALWAYS KEEP BONSAI SOIL MOIST. Water every day but do not soak the tree, as this will rot the fragile root system. Keep the tree outside, moving it to a sheltered spot over the winter, away from harsh winds.

A BRIEF HISTORY OF BONSAI

The Chinese first created the miniature landscapes during the Han Dynasty (206 BC–220 AD), and called the art *penjing*. Miniaturized gardening was introduced to Japan by Buddhist monks during the Heian period (794–1191 AD) and became known as *bonsai* – 'tray planting'. For many years it was a nobleman's privilege and was on the verge of dying out when the Chinese invaded in the fourteenth century. Thereafter its popularity grew amongst all classes in Japan and the art was gradually refined.

The first major bonsai exhibition in the West was held in London in 1909, but it wasn't until 1935 that soldiers returning from Japan with bonsai in tow sparked widespread interest in the art. The trees they brought back soon died, but not before Westerners had seen enough to want to learn to cultivate bonsai gardens of their own.

CHAPTER FIVE

GARDENS

*The great gardens of England so generously thrown open
to the public through the summer to help the Queen's nurses,
never fail to fill the foreigner with an admiration that surpasses
even the admiration he feels for our landscape.*

SPB MAIS

SOMETHING FOR THE WEEKEND

VISITING GARDENS is a national pastime for gardeners and is one of the backbones of *Gardeners' World*.

Every programme has at least one garden, nursery or national collection in it. We meet enthusiastic gardeners, passionate plantsmen and avid collectors and, over the years, hundreds have been featured – so many that we sometimes wonder if the pot will one day be empty. But it never is. Every day we find a new garden or a new gardener and, every time we do, our own love of gardening is rekindled.

A WORD ABOUT THE YELLOW BOOK. This guide to the 3500 or so mostly private gardens open to the public under the National Gardens Scheme is indispensable to any garden visitor. It is packed with details of all sorts of gardens open throughout the year, but is particularly renowned for its small gardens. For a small admission charge you can get to see the best gardens in the country. These are the perfect places to find inspiration: all are packed with ideas and many sell some of the plants growing in the gardens.

THE ROYAL HORTICULTURAL SOCIETY (RHS) GARDENS at Wisley, Surrey; Hyde Hall, Essex; Harlow Carr, North Yorkshire; and Rosemoor, Devon, are worth visiting at any time of year and are specifically laid out to inspire and educate. The different locations of the gardens are also invaluable in demonstrating to gardeners what plants will thrive in their specific areas of the country. Look out for particular events and educational walks and talks.

NURSERIES ARE NUMEROUS and many have gardens attached to them where you can see the plants growing. Some gardeners have been known to have nursery-visiting holidays around the country. An invaluable companion to nursery visiting is *The Plant Finder,* which is produced (and updated annually) by the RHS and lists every plant available in the UK and where it can be bought. Even so, if you are looking for a particular plant, it is a good idea to ring ahead to see if it is available. So much plant knowledge can be gleaned from experienced nurserymen and women that visits are almost compulsory!

SO, IF YOU ARE SETTING OUT for the first time on the journey that is gardening, then our strongest recommendation is to visit as many gardens as you can. Take notes, take pictures and never be afraid to copy a successful plant combination or design feature. As you progress in gardening and become more confident, your garden will become your own original creation and, who knows, one day it may be open to the public and *Gardeners' World* will come and visit you!

THE BEST GARDENS IN THE COUNTRY are far too numerous to mention but here are some 'must be visited' ones that won't fail to inspire – they certainly impressed us!

WINTER GARDENS

Anglesey Abbey
Lode, Cambridge
Cambridgeshire
CB25 9EJ
T: 01223 810080
W: www.angleseyabbey.
org

Hodsock Priory
Blyth near Worksop
Nottinghamshire
S81 0TY
T: 01909 591 204
W: www.snowdrops.co.uk

**Cambridge University
Botanic Garden**
1 Brookside
Cambridge
Cambridgeshire
CB2 1JE
T: 01223 336265
W: www.botanic.cam.
ac.uk

**Sir Harold Hillier
Gardens & Arboretum**
Jermyns Lane
Ampfield, Romsey
Hampshire SO51 0QA
T: 01794 368787
W: www.hilliergardens.
org.uk

SPRING GARDENS

Marwood Hill Gardens
Marwood, Barnstaple
Devon, EX31 4EB
T: 01271 342528
W: www.
marwoodhillgarden.co.uk

Broadleigh Gardens
Bishops Hull

Taunton, Somerset
TA4 1AE
T: 01823 286231
W: www.broadleighbulbs.
co.uk/gardens.htm

RHS Garden Wisley
Woking GU23 6QB
T: 0845 2609000
W: www.rhs.org.uk/
gardens/wisely

Glendurgan Garden
Mawnan Smith
near Falmouth
Cornwall, TR11 5JZ
T: 01326 250906
W: www.nationaltrust.
org.uk

**Antony Woodland
Garden**
Antony House
Torpoint, Cornwall
PL11 2QA
T: 01752 812191
W: www.nationaltrust.
org.uk

SUMMER GARDENS

Sissinghurst Castle
Sissinghurst
near Cranbrook
Kent, TN17 2AB
T: 01580 710701
W: www.nationaltrust.
org.uk

Great Dixter
Northiam, Rye,
East Sussex, TN31 6PH
T: 01797 252878
W: www.greatdixter.co.uk

Hidcote Manor
Hidcote Bartrim
near Chipping Campden

Gloucestershire
GL55 6LR
T: 01386 438333
W: www.nationaltrust.
org.uk

Arley Hall & Gardens
Northwich, Cheshire
CW9 6NA
T: 01565 777353
W: www.
arleyhallandgardens.com

**East Ruston
Old Vicarage**
East Ruston, Norwich,
Norfolk, NR12 9HN
T: 01692 650432
W: www.e-ruston-
oldvicaragegardens.co.uk

West Dean Gardens
West Dean, Chichester
West Sussex, PO18 0QZ
T: 01243 811301
W: www.westdean.org.uk/
site/gardens

The Abbey House
Malmesbury
Wiltshire, SN16 9AS
T: 01666 822212
W: www.
abbeyhousegardens.co.uk

AUTUMN GARDENS

Knoll Gardens
Hampreston
Wimborne BH21 7ND
T: 01202 873931
W: enquiries@knoll
gardens.co.uk

**Pensthorpe Nature
Reserve and Gardens**
prairie-style planting
Pensthorpe, Fakenham

Norfolk NR21 0LN
T: 01328 851465
W: www.pensthorpe.com

Westonbirt, the National Arboretum
Tetbury
Gloucestershire
GL8 8QS
T: 01666 880220
W: www.forestry.gov.uk/
westonbirt

Bluebell Arboretum and Nursery
Annwell Lane
Smisby, Ashby de la
Zouch, Leicestershire
LE65 2TA
T: 01530 413 700
W: www.bluebellnursery.
com

The Picton Garden
(National Collection
of Michaelmas daisies)
Colwall, Malvern
Worcestershire
WR13 6QE
T: 01684 540416

Waterperry Gardens
(late-flowering
herbaceous border)
near Wheatley,
Oxfordshire, OX33 1JZ
T: 01844 339254
W: www.waterperry
gardens.co.uk

ROSE GARDENS

David Austin Roses
Bowling Green Lane,
Albrighton,
Wolverhampton
WV7 3HB
www.davidaustinroses.
com

Mottisfont Abbey Garden
Mottisfont, near Romsey
Hampshire, SO51 0LP
T: 01794 341220
W: www.nationaltrust.
org.uk

Peter Beales Roses
London Road
Attleborough
Norfolk, NR17 1AY
T: 01953 454707
W: www.classicroses.co.uk

Mannington Gardens
Mannington Hall
Saxthorpe, Norwich
NR11 7BB
T: 01263 584175
W: www.
manningtongardens.
co.uk

HERB GARDENS

Chesters Walled Garden
Chollerford
Hexham
Northumberland
NE46 4BQ
T: 01434 681483
W: www.
chesterswalledgarden.
fsnet.co.uk

The Walled Garden
(see The Yellow Book
for open days, or call to
make an appointment)
6 Rose Terrace, off Fort
Royal Hill, Worcester
WR5 1BU
T: 01905 354 629

Acorn Bank Garden and Watermill
Temple Sowerby
Penrith, Cumbria

CA10 1SP
T: 017683 61893
W: www.nationaltrust.
org.uk

The National Herb Centre
Banbury Road
Warmington
Warwickshire
OX17 1DF
T: 01295 690999
W: www.herbcentre.co.uk

DESIGN

Broughton Grange Walled Garden
(designed by Tom Stuart
Smith. Check *The Yellow
Book* for opening times)
Wykeham Lane
Broughton, Oxfordshire
T: 01295 252044

Lance Hattatt Design Garden
(book ahead)
Ledgemoor, Weobley
Herefordshire
T: 01544 318468

Bury Court
Bentley, near Farnham
Surrey, GU10 5LZ
T: 01420 23202
W: www.burycourtbarn.
co.uk

Denmans
Fontwell, Arundel
West Sussex, BN18 0SU
T: 01243 542808
W: www.denmans-
garden.co.uk

Little Sparta
Dunsyre, near Lanark
Lanarkshire, ML11 8NG

Scotland
W: www.littlesparta.co.uk

The Manor House, Upton Grey
(Gertrude Jekyll garden. Book ahead)
The Manor House, Upton Grey
Hampshire, RG25 2RD
T: 01256 862827
W: www. gertrudejekyllgarden. co.uk

VEGETABLE GARDENS

Tatton Park
(restored kitchen garden but much more besides)
Knutsford, Cheshire
WA16 6QN
T: 01625 374435
W: www.tattonpark.org.uk

Audley End Organic Kitchen Garden
Saffron Walden
Essex, CB11 4JG
T: 01799 522148
W: www.english-heritage. org.uk/audleyend

CONTAINER GARDENS

Whichford Pottery
Whichford
near Shipston-on-Stour
Warwickshire
CV36 5PG
T: 01608 684416
W: www. whichfordpottery.com

ORGANIC GARDENS

Garden Organic Ryton
Coventry
Warwickshire
United Kingdom
CV8 3LG
T: 02476 303517
W: www.gardenorganic. org.uk/gardens/ryton. php

ACKNOWLEDGMENTS

Louise Hampden would like to thank the presenters, researchers and staff of *Gardeners' World* for their love of the programme and their love of gardening – a day with any of them is full of marvellous gardening stories, tips and hints. In particular, my thanks to Dr Claire Johnson and Russell Jordan for their help in ensuring the correctness of the tips in this book.

BBC Books would like to thank the following for permission to use material for this book:

David Austin *The English Roses* (Conran Octopus, 2005); Fern Marshall Bradley & Jane Courtier *The Complete Vegetable Gardener* (The Reader's Digest, 2006); Beth Chatto *Beth Chatto's Green Tapestry* (Collins, 1989); Monty Don *The Complete Gardener* (Dorling Kindersley, 2003); Margery Fish *A Flower for Every Day* (Capital Books, 1965); Geoff Hamilton *Geoff Hamilton's Paradise Gardens* (BBC Books, 1997); Dr D G Hessayon *The Container Expert* (Expert Books, 2007); M James *The Complete Guide to Home Gardens* (Associated Newspapers); Jonathan Keyte, in *Gardening With the Experts*, Rachel de Thame (ed) (BBC Books, 2003); Joy Larkcom *Grow Your Own Vegetables* (Frances Lincoln, 2002); Christopher Lloyd *The Well-Tempered Garden*, Cassell Plc., a division of The Orion Publishing Group (London); S P B Mais introduction to *The Complete Guide to Home Gardens* (Associated Newspapers); Dan Pearson *The Garden* (Ebury Press, 2001); Richard Rosenfeld *Containers For Patios* (Dorling Kindersley 2007); Gay Search *Gardening without a Garden* (Dorling Kindersley, 1997); Rachel de Thame *Star Plants* (BBC Books, 2002); Alan Titchmarsh *How to be a Gardener* (BBC Books, 2002); *How to be a Gardener: Secrets of Success* (BBC Books, 2003); *The Gardener's Year* (BBC Books, 2005).

All original illustrations © Christoph Mett.